AF374796

BRIDGING TOMORROW'S KNOWLEDGE GAP WITH AI:

Transforming Education for the Future

INGRID SEABRA

NONSUCH MEDIA PTE. LTD.

First published in English in 2023 by Nonsuch Media Pte. Ltd

nonsuchmedia.com

Title: Bridging Tomorrow's Knowledge Gap with AI: Transforming Education for the Future

Author: Ingrid Seabra

Editor: A. Lee

Book Cover By: Elisa Reis for Nonsuch Media Pte. Ltd.

Graphic Design: Elisa Reis for Nonsuch Media Pte. Ltd.

Copyright for the first English edition © 2023 Nonsuch Media Pte. Ltd.

ISBN: 979-8-89214-045-4

The author has made every effort to provide accurate information at the time of publication; however, neither the publisher nor the author assume any responsibility for errors or changes that may occur after publication.

Furthermore, the publisher has no control over and assumes no responsibility for third-party authors or websites or their content.

Learning is more than just the key to escaping the prison of igno-
rance; it is a journey of self-discovery and evolution. Learning unlocks
the freedom to choose and opens our minds to the interplay between
the known and the unknown, illuminating paths to endless possibilities.

—Ingrid Seabra

CONTENTS

INTRODUCTION

After spending several years in the corporate world, I decided to follow my passion for education and become a teacher. It has been an intensely rewarding, albeit challenging, journey since day one. One hurdle I did not anticipate was contending with the distractions of technology and shortened attention spans among students.

This situation made me question whether I was doing something incorrectly or if the increasing presence of "digital natives" in the classrooms called for a different approach. Reflecting on this, I realized that teaching had evolved, and I needed to adapt to continue enriching my students' learning experiences. I grappled with a pressing question: "How can I make education more stimulating and engaging for students?" A number of factors contributed to this complexity, such as societal changes due to the prevalence of social media and the introduction of new teaching methods, notably in STEM (Science, Technology, Engineering, and Mathematics) subjects.

Upon deep reflection, I concluded that changing the curriculum and reevaluating my role within the classroom was of utmost importance. This involved managing student behavior and providing feedback at various stages of their learning journey. It is a complex process, as each student has unique needs across various dimensions that must be addressed. Embracing these differences and learning from their perspectives became my strategy. In an era where students seek personalized attention and resist rigid structures, I surmised that this shift might be linked to the influence of new technologies, prompting further exploration.

I am sure many educators can relate to my challenges. It is no easy task. The realm of teaching presents daily difficulties for everyone involved—administrators grappling with budgets, teachers and parents seeking resources and answers, and students navigating an unprecedented era.

Teaching can be confusing and occasionally frustrating, especially when today's students favor the independence that modern tech tools offer over traditional teacher-led instruction. Consequently, I had to reassess the skills and knowledge necessary to deliver effective education and maintain student engagement. I noticed increased student attention when I shifted to a more individualized approach. Implementing this change required significant dedication and effort, but it was a game-changer in my teaching journey.

In this book, I aim to explore the impact and reasons behind these disruptive educational changes. I also aspire to reflect on the future of teaching. The integration of technology in education has transformed us in unimaginable ways. Along with these advancements comes great responsibility. As we progress, we must consider how to harness these changes to enhance educational outcomes and prepare our students for the future.

As we navigate through an increasingly digital world without borders, educators must be prepared to adapt and evolve. However, amidst these changes, important questions arise: What will become of teachers? How can we ensure that their expertise remains appreciated and utilized? How can schools facilitate a smoother transition for those who have dedicated their lives to nurturing future leaders?

While far from perfect, it is vital to recognize that the current educational system has faced challenges for some time. Persistent issues have plagued the system for decades, yet they seem resistant to resolution due to bureaucracy and the politics of altering the status quo. This book explores the potential role of Artificial Intelligence

(AI) in disrupting this stagnant system, making schools more effective and efficient while addressing long-standing concerns.

Moreover, I delve into how teachers and students leverage AI in their classrooms. By examining the benefits and potential pitfalls of integrating AI into education, I aim to provide a balanced perspective. Furthermore, I explore emerging technologies, such as augmented reality (AR) and machine learning algorithms, which are poised to shape our future classrooms.

I firmly believe that personalized education holds the key to unleashing the potential of the next generation. As technology continues its rapid evolution, its impact permeates all aspects of society, including education. Thus, staying abreast of the latest technological innovations becomes imperative, particularly for those teaching computer science and STEM subjects. My experience teaching these subjects has underscored the importance of keeping up to date with advancements in the field.

This book is a product of my reflections and inquiries into the future of education. I recognized the need for change and embarked on a journey to understand its potential impact on teachers and students. We live in a time when technology is reshaping the world at an unprecedented pace. The advent of transformative technologies like AI heralds a new era, promising to alter our lives profoundly.

While AI has been around for some time, it is only recently begun to disrupt industries like education. In this book, I discuss why AI could solve many of our educational challenges and how it might forever change the education landscape.

The pursuit of understanding the future of education is a complex endeavor, fraught with detours and diversions. Throughout this book, there will be moments where it becomes necessary to recalibrate thoughts, ideas, and opinions due to the intricacies of the content. While certain viewpoints may initially appear contradictory, a closer look often reveals underlying similarities. It is crucial to approach such a vast topic with an open mind, recognizing that our actions and thoughts today inevitably shape the future of education.

CHAPTER 1

Artificial Intelligence (AI)

Before we delve into the topic, let us first define artificial intelligence. Often abbreviated as "AI," it encompasses the theory and development of computer systems that mimic human intelligence. This includes visual perception, speech recognition, decision-making, and language translation capabilities. In essence, machine learning, a subset of AI, can be defined as a method by which computer software improves performance on specific tasks without being explicitly programmed. Instead, improvements are made based on examples of correct responses and their causes.

The term artificial intelligence has been circulating since 1956, marking the dawn of an era where machines or sophisticated software began to display intelligence.[1] This enabled them to perform tasks and solve problems previously considered exclusive to human intellect. Today, AI is employed across various industries, including health care, finance, and education.

The transformative potential of AI is immense. It promises to alter our interaction with information in ways that could significantly reshape society. However, to integrate AI seamlessly into our lives, we must address many challenges that could profoundly impact education and the community.

---

[1]. Strickland, E., "The turbulent past and uncertain future of Artificial Intelligence" 2021, (https://spectrum.ieee.org/history-of-ai).

Artificial intelligence represents the next monumental technological leap, one that is sweeping across the globe. Yet, the rapid pace of this evolution presents a challenge as humans struggle to adapt quickly enough due to insufficient preparation time. And we are not just talking about computers here; even everyday devices like cell phones are becoming increasingly intelligent. They can now perform various tasks, from making restaurant reservations to predicting election outcomes.

In conclusion, as we stand on the brink of an AI-driven era, it is crucial to understand and prepare for the changes this technology will bring. Doing so can ensure we harness its full potential while mitigating adverse impacts.

The intelligence of AI

Artificial intelligence is often categorized into general and exceptional intelligence. While the division is a subject of debate in human intelligence, the parallels drawn with AI have been instrumental in deepening our understanding of intelligence as a concept. Rather than perceiving intelligence as a unified entity, emerging scientific evidence suggests that it is more accurately defined as a combination of various independent abilities. This complexity becomes evident when considering artificial intelligence from a cognitive perspective.

However, specialists in the AI field grapple with more intricate issues. They are tasked with answering complex questions such as "What precisely defines intelligence?" and "What are the unique domains of intelligence?"

People regularly categorize intelligence, and one might wonder why this is the case. Portrayals of AI in science fiction movies depict extraordinary cognitive capabilities, implying that AI can accomplish virtually anything. However, AI typically assumes a more mundane role.

Consider the ubiquitous smartphone, for example. Many people begin their day interacting with AI through their smartphones. Despite this being an obvious manifestation of AI in our daily lives, its significance often goes unnoticed. These compact devices, which we carry around all day, are repositories of artificial intelligence. They perform tasks ranging from the simple, like setting alarms, to the complex, underscoring the pervasive influence of AI in our daily lives.

Hence, AI plays a crucial role in our daily responsibilities, but it is important to note that not all AI functions similarly. For instance, some AI helps navigate traffic using GPS, satellite imaging, intelligent traffic lights, and traffic reports. Some AI, embedded in image processing software, captures license plates in split seconds. The camera software has grown increasingly intelligent on mobile phones, enabling even the most photographically challenged individuals to take decent shots.

The AI decision-making process, which adjusts light settings and distances in response to environmental factors, has made this remarkable achievement possible. Even when a photo seems ruined, AI can transform it into a masterpiece. In massively multiplayer online (MMO) games, AI processors streamline game performance and enhance the overall experience. Games generate obstacles and opponents tailored to different difficulty levels, abilities, and playing styles, ensuring players remain engaged.

Given these advancements, it is natural to expect the integration of optimal challenges into educational systems through artificial intelligence and hyperspectral imaging (HI). History provides numerous examples of such integrations. Consider Akinator, a mind-reading game that AI powers. The game, founded on fuzzy logic, allows values other than true and false binary options. This technique is also used in washing machines, aiding with daily chores. These diverse applications demonstrate that AI usage varies in processing efficiency, but specialization invariably enhances AI performance.

Chatbots represent a more advanced system of artificial intelligence. They are so sophisticated that it is sometimes difficult to discern who is on the other end of the line—human or machine. Similarly, search engines, recommendation systems, and filters have streamlined our lives by offering a better understanding of what we want, why we want it, and how to get it. We do not have to think; AI thinks for us.

Moreover, these AI systems are designed to gather and analyze data, predicting our habits and lifestyles. Elon Musk, the present-day visionary of next-generation technological development, audaciously proposes that we might communicate our desires through chips within five to ten years.[2]

While it may seem that Musk's projections venture into the realm of science fiction, they are not entirely unfounded. The rise of touch gestures and voice control capabilities in contemporary smartphones signifies a shift toward advanced methods of communication. Besides the system's processing power, the efficiency level and task load capabilities of artificial intelligence primarily revolve around the design and intention of the creators.

Artificial intelligence strives to replicate complex cognitive processes through artificial means. Artificial narrow intelligence (ANI), a subset of AI, employs specialized algorithms to perform specific tasks more efficiently than humans do. For instance, computerized brain translators or image recognition systems can flawlessly transform one language into another. This narrow focus ensures accuracy by preventing the system from venturing beyond the scope of translation, which could lead to errors.[3]

The game of chess exemplifies the limitless potential of AI. In 1997, IBM's Deep Blue defeated world chess champion Garry Kasparov, demonstrating AI's superior decision-making ability in games with well-defined rules. Further advancements were seen when IBM's Watson system outperformed human champions on Jeopardy! in 2011, and Google's AlphaGo defeated South Korean Go champion Lee

---

[2]. Musk, E., "Joe Rogan Experience" #1470, 2020, J. Rogan, Interviewer.

[3]. Narrow Artificial Intelligence, "What is Narrow Artificial Intelligence (Narrow AI)?" Definition from Techopedia, 2022, (https://www.techopedia.com/definition/32874/narrow-artificial-intelligence-narrow-ai#:~:text=Narrow%20artificial%20intelligence%20%28narrow%20AI%29%20is%20a%20specific,will%20not%20automatically%20be%20applied%20to%20other%20tasks).

Sedol in 2016.[4] These victories underscore AI's capacity to process and store information rapidly, making strategic decisions that often outsmart human opponents.

In contrast, artificial general intelligence (AGI) aims to match human cognitive abilities. It embodies a comprehensive range of mental capabilities akin to human intelligence, including pattern recognition, logic, information storage, language interpretation, learning, abstraction, communication, decision-making, perception, and problem-solving. It might encompass auxiliary human abilities such as empathy and creativity. However, despite significant research, achieving AGI remains an elusive goal.[5]

Artificial superintelligence (ASI) is a hypothetical future form of AI that surpasses all aspects of human intelligence. It could potentially undergo recursive self-improvement, leading to a machine intelligence explosion or "intelligence singularity." This has led some AI proponents to speculate that once ASI is developed, it could become uncontrollable and pose an existential threat to humanity.

Artificial superintelligence is postulated to be superior to human intelligence in specific areas, including socioemotional ability, creativity, and wisdom. However, the development of ASI is uncertain. Robert Trappl, the director of the Austrian Research Institute for Artificial Intelligence, has stated: "At present, an Artificial Intelligence must be better at certain niche things than humans...but I regard the development of a superintelligence...as highly improbable."[6]

Thus, creating an AI system that surpasses human intelligence may not be workable. We can strive to develop innovative, programmable strategies that perform dedicated tasks with precision. Such

---

4. Machine Learning Knowledge, "5 Epic Times when AI defeated Human Champions in Games" 2019, (https://machinelearningknowledge.ai/epic-times-when-ai-defeated-humans-champions-in-games/).

5. Senior, J. and Gyarmathy, É., *AI and Developing Human Intelligence*, (2 Park Square, Milton Park, Abingdon, Oxon OX14 4RN: Routledge, 2022), p. 81.

6. Trappl, R., "Programs can do everything that humans can - and more" 2015, Futurezone, Interviewer.

systems will help us keep pace with the times and maintain relevance in a rapidly evolving technological landscape.

The flexibility of intelligence

A French psychologist named Alfred Binet, one of the most influential psychologists in history, created the first widely used intelligence test. After being commissioned by France's Ministry of Education, he developed the instrument to identify school kids who needed helpful studies with his collaborating partner, Theodore Simon. His collaboration with Theodore Simon led them to create the Binet-Simon Intelligence Scale, one of today's most available tools for measuring cognitive functioning.[7]

The Stanford-Binet intelligence test is a cognitive test of tasks assessing an individual's mathematical skills, memory, and spatial perception abilities. The results of the Stanford-Binet are often used to identify individuals who may be gifted or have learning disabilities. The test is still in use today, though it has been updated and revised several times since its inception. The latest version of the Stanford-Binet was released in 2003. Intelligence tests such as the Stanford-Binet are essential for measuring an individual's cognitive abilities.[8] However, it is essential to note that intelligence tests are not perfect measures of intelligence. They often do not consider an individual's emotional intelligence or social intelligence. Additionally, elements like motivation and anxiety can have an impact on the results of intelligence tests. Despite these limitations, intelligence tests remain valuable for assessing cognitive abilities.[9]

---

[7]. Wikipedia.org, "Stanford-Binet Intelligence Scales" 2021, (https://en.wikipedia.org/wiki/Stanford%E2%80%93Binet_Intelligence_Scales).

[8]. Ranjha, A., "Intelligence Test – An Overview of Stanford-Binet Intelligence Test" (https://psychologyroots.com/intelligence-test-an-overview-of-stanford-binet-intelligence-test/).

[9]. Whitten, A., "Do IQ. Tests Actually Measure Intelligence?" 2020, (https://www.discovermagazine.com/mind/do-iq-tests-actually-measure-intelligence).

It has been the primary system for determining what we define as human intelligence, otherwise known as intelligence quotient (IQ). At the time, artificial intelligence was only a tall dream still conceived in science fiction. Towards the end of the twentieth century, engineers and neuroscientists joined forces, driven by the concept of neural learning, despite the differences in their respective disciplines.

Over time, thinking about the idea of cognitive ability turned into a multidisciplinary topic that gave rise to a number of fields that overlap and build on each other. These fields blur, narrow, clarify, expand, and develop the idea of intelligence. Think of it as a lab rat poked and prodded by everyone in a lab, regardless of their inclinations.

Intelligence and other surrounding matters

The concept of intelligence was attributed to Plato and Aristotle by Sir Cyril Burt in 1955. Cicero is credited with coining the term.[10] It has been a subject of thought since antiquity and probably before, although there is no documentation to back it up. In Aristotle's view, reason defined the human capacity to rein in our basic animal instincts, and modern society is struggling to exercise that kind of restraint.

Burt made more pronounced distinctions on the subject regarding Charles Darwin's era. The theory of evolution designed how humans pictured themselves. Darwin also dabbled in reason, which he categorized into levels and was more of a situation of some people being more reasonable than others. He posited that "mental powers" manifest strongly in more advanced species from his evolutionary perspective.[11]

---

[10]. Hamsher, K., "Intelligence and Aphasia" 2007, (https://doi.org/10.1016/B978-012619322-0/50013-0).

[11]. Darwin, C. "The origin of species by means of natural selection, or the preservation of favored races in the struggle for life. In C. Darwin, the origin of species by means of natural selection, or the preservation of favored races in the struggle for life." (London: John Murray, 1872), p. 181.

In 1893, George Romanes, one of Darwin's acquaintances, authored a book on the mental evolution of animals in which he discussed animal intelligence. Around this time, intelligence came to refer to phenomena that eluded full comprehension or existed beyond our current conceptualization. The concept was probably unaccepted for a while. And not without good reasons. It is innate to create something from our imaginations and make it a part of the shared, accepted reality. Intersubjective entities within this zone of shared accepted facts include social norms, money, religion, companies, etcetera.

None of these entities can exist without the beliefs of a large body of people. Furthermore, it makes sense. For Christianity to exist, for instance, people must believe in the Christian God and the dogmas of the faith. However, for companies to continue to exist, people must believe in their products and services to part with their money. Yuval Harari, a philosopher and historian, suggests that the vast impact and success of Homo sapiens primarily stem from their capacity to create shared myths, thereby guiding large groups of humans in various directions.[12]

As far as we know, no other species can digest or believe the imaginary stories we tell ourselves. Not even our ancestors, the Homo erectus, who lived for nearly two million years and only faded out during the onset of Homo sapiens, could believe these stories. Taking it further back, not even Neanderthals, who have proved to be more intelligent than we initially gave them credit, would accept. Incidentally, however, the extinction of the previous two human species could likely be due to the activities of Homo sapiens, whose extraordinary mental power is likely the ability to paint and maintain an intersubjective reality rather than intelligence. As a result, the masses can be influenced, and this cognitive ability is the outcome of faith as it is about reason.

---

[12]. Harari, Y. N., *Sapiens: A Brief History of Humankind.* (Signal Books, 2014), p.35.

For example, Harari describes this concept as the "cognitive revolution"—the victory of human intelligence. In turn, it presents intersubjective reality as an introduction to faith's role in cognition.

A provocative line of thought is that our ability to believe a story or myth could be more of a decline in reason than any intellectual achievement. However, it is a fundamental thought, mainly as science aims to connect our fate with astonishing cognitive capacity, even though many factors define intelligence as a secondary function in the behavior of Homo sapiens. People considered highly intelligent are not so different from people with low or average intelligence in many ways, including:

- These concepts are essential to understanding the human mind, as creativity allows us to solve problems innovatively. Emotional responses make us human and connect us. In turn, intersubjective reality is necessary for gossip and spreading fake news. Intuitive thinking can be quick or slow depending on the situation, and animalistic tendencies often drive our decision-making.
- On the other hand, cognitive schemata help us understand the world, and implementation is critical to achieving success. These concepts are essential to understanding how we think and decide, and each contributes to our overall understanding of human cognition.
- There is a fine line between wisdom, information, data, and knowledge. However, in day-to-day life, people regularly do not concern themselves with the semantics of these differences and will navigate any situation using these concepts. In comparison, artificial intelligence is independent of these phenomena, contributing to human errors. It can be argued that such straightforward, unrelenting cognitive operation has a downside. A machine without motivation, emotions, or instincts does not rely on them to process thoughts. Its only inclination is to tap into the wealth of information and data

that feeds its knowledge. However, false data will also cause the cognition of artificial intelligence to turn out wrong.

- Task-centricity can also be problematic when artificial intelligence cannot comprehend considerations outside its direct instructions. Blind commitment to following commands is also a human trait that can worsen subjective factors. Furthermore, since we cannot accurately define how these factors relate to intelligence, we cannot categorize human history as an achievement story. It would mean that intelligence is the foundation of our success, but it would also mean that our cognitive abilities, especially intersubjective realities, are as essential as intelligence. On the contrary, faith plays a more prominent role here than thinking. For one, we cannot truly claim success when we have endangered our existence and harmed a sizable portion of our environment in just a few hundred thousand years.

Suppose we calculate the measure of a species' success based on its survivability. In that case, we cannot indeed postulate that other species have not been far more successful than we are or could ever be. For instance, cockroaches have existed for almost three hundred million years; the saber tooth tiger outlived the Homo erectus, which was around for some two million years. Yet until now, Homo sapiens have failed to rid themselves of the annoying bugs that are roaches. So, how do we define our success or intelligence?

Artificial, human, and universal intelligences

One of the most straightforward platforms for exploring our intelligence comes from examining the various subtypes of artificial intelligence (AI). Despite being a topic of ongoing conversation and debate, the definition of AI has maintained relative consistency across literature and media over the years. This consistency starkly contrasts human intelligence, imbued with many subjective meanings and conceptualizations dating back several millennia.

Exploring intelligence from a broader, potentially universal perspective could be another effective approach if such a concept exists. For instance, a theoretical framework of universal intelligence could offer a balanced platform for comparing various cognitive factors. Furthermore, this system could prove instrumental in enhancing our understanding of human cognitive capacity, enabling us to more effectively categorize and comprehend the roles and significance of different types of intelligence.

By placing AI and human intelligence within this context, we may discover new insights into the intricate complexity of cognition, further closing the gap between the artificial and the natural, the machine and the human.

CHAPTER 2

Education

Flaws in the traditional system of education

The current educational system is frequently criticized for its perceived inability to engage students, impart real-world skills and knowledge, and cultivate critical thinking. This chapter delves into some of these issues and explores the possible flaws within our education system. For instance, the absence of clear guidelines for successful teaching and learning, or the lack of a universally accepted contemporary theory of education, suggests that our educational system is far from perfect.

In the traditional educational model, students are often restricted to classrooms for extended periods. Teachers typically deliver lectures while students passively listen and take notes, a process that can be monotonous. The lack of collaborative activities hinders peer-to-peer learning and the exchange of ideas. Moreover, textbooks may present rigid information, compelling teachers to promote a single perspective on topics, leaving little room for exploring diverse viewpoints.

The shortcomings of the traditional educational system become more apparent when viewed through the lens of a teacher. First, teachers frequently grapple with insufficient planning time, leading to last-minute changes that may not cater to students' needs. Second, the lack of scope for innovation in teaching methods can render education monotonous and uninspiring. Third, student engagement levels are frequently low as digital platforms increasingly outshine physical sources of information.

Another significant drawback is the curriculum's rigidity, which limits students to prescribed topics instead of fostering their broader interests. Critics argue that this approach stifles intellectual growth. Indeed, many students only begin to discover new interests once they reach college or enter the workforce.

Traditional teaching methods can also inhibit the development of leadership skills, a crucial aspect of careers involving robust social interactions. Instead of molding students into conforming individuals, we should inspire them to become independent thinkers capable of making informed decisions. Cultivating leadership skills empowers students to make choices that will positively impact their future careers and communities. Hence, conventional teaching methods cannot foster increasingly sought-after skills in today's professional landscape.

Education flaws in Europe

Europe has a long way to go regarding social cohesion, economic growth, and prosperity. Inequality still exists in Europe today, largely due to the education system. Those who come from less privileged backgrounds are not taken into consideration, leading to poverty and reduced job prospects for future generations.

Inequality within these areas can be seen as both an external threat and a potential problem-solving tool by focusing more on corrective measures rather than beneficiary assistance without fundamental change.[13]

What concerns me is the fact that investment in education is decreasing. The Lifelong Learning Platform (LLLP) has compiled a Eu-

---

[13]. "Education and training in Europe: inequality remains a challenge" Brussels: European Commission, 2017, (https://ec.europa.eu/commission/presscorner/detail/en/IP_17_4261).

ropean education spending database. The data shows that, while European countries invested heavily in their educational systems at one point, they are now down.[14]

The data shows that while some countries are making strides in investing more in education, others continue to decrease. The three highest increase percentages of investment came from Belgium at +0.1 percent, Sweden with an increment of only one-tenth percent but still positive outcomes, and Croatia with +1.7 percent. All the other twenty-five countries decreased their investment.

The European countries that have not implemented fiscal consolidation measures face the consequences of their debt crisis. They seem to think education and training programs will be easy to cut, despite how important it is for them as a country to recover from such economic hardship. Europe has witnessed an embarrassing decline in education expenditures over the last decade. From 5 percent of GDP spent on average per student back when Europe was centralized, now it is only 4–4.7 percent.[15] The situation is distressing, and the shrinking funding for education hurts all its sectors. It also decreases personal development and skilled labor availability in society and benefits from learning itself, leading to an even bigger problem. If left unchecked, those who cannot afford higher costs go unmatched by public funds due to their lower percentage destined toward having access to post-secondary institutions or training programs that would help them catch up.

To maintain our competitive edge in the worldwide economy, we must prioritize increasing our investment in education. Indeed, our future prosperity hinges on it. Learning is not merely a necessity but a fundamental human right that should be universally accessible.

---

14. Media & Learning, "Europe's Budget for Education and Training at Its Lowest" 2020, (https://media-and-learning.eu/type/news/europes-budget-for-education-and-training-at-its-lowest/).

15. Lifelong Learning Platform (LLLP), "Europe's share of GDP for education and training has never been this low. A comparative analysis" 2020, (https://lllplatform.eu/news/europes-share-of-gdp-for-education-and-training-has-never-been-this-low-a-comparative-analysis-investment-education-eurostat/).

The intricacies of European education may seem elusive to many of us. However, striving for a deeper understanding of this system is crucial. Intriguing developments in this region's educational landscape warrant our attention and exploration. By broadening our perspective, we can glean valuable insights and discover innovative strategies to enhance our educational practices.

The Europeanization of education systems is a new development. Theoretically, it should be the responsibility of member states: Education in Europe has always been confined to nation-state levels, but with such enormous differences. One could hardly call any single version better than another or even relevant across all countries on this continent where different traditions are strong. The differences in language between geographic regions can be considered nothing more than the result of history, which has led many people living in Europe until 1992 to hold on firmly to their native tongue and single teaching customs. But in 1992, the Maastricht Treaty forced all European countries to adopt specific universal standards regarding how they teach courses across curriculums ranging from pre-kindergarten to college graduation. It was a direct response to the fact that, as industries increasingly globalized their workforces, companies were finding it challenging to train personnel from different educational backgrounds to work together efficiently.[16]

The Bologna Process's introduction marked a pivotal moment in this pact, aiming to standardize European Higher Education and align it more closely with other international education systems. This initiative has streamlined the process for students to transfer credits between countries and ensured their degrees are mutually recognized. It has significantly enhanced labor mobility within Europe and bolstered the EU's competitiveness in the global economy.

While the Bologna Process has achieved notable success, it has its challenges. One of the most significant criticisms leveled against it is

---

[16]. "The Europeanization of schooling: what is a European Education?" OpenDemocracy Press, 2018, (https://www.opendemocracy.net/en/can-europe-make-it/europeanization-of-schooling/).

that it has led to the homogenization of European higher education. This uniformity implies that students across different countries are being taught the same subjects in identical manners, leading to concerns about losing diversity and creativity in the educational system. The unique characteristics and innovative teaching methods that once distinguished various European educational institutions risk being diluted under this standardized approach.

Therefore, while the Bologna Process has undeniably brought significant benefits, there remains a need for ongoing evaluation and refinement to ensure it does not compromise the richness and diversity of European education.

Another challenge the Bologna Process presents is the escalating cost of higher education. Universities have been compelled to invest in new infrastructure and expand their staff to accommodate the demand for more standardized courses. This increased expenditure has strained public budgets, leading to a general decline in European educational investment. While the Bologna Process has had its share of adverse consequences, it is crucial to remember that it was implemented in response to an existing issue. On balance, it has largely accomplished its objectives.

A significant part of the problem lies in our outdated educational infrastructure, designed for the twentieth century, struggling to meet the demands of the twenty-first-century global economy. To stay competitive, we need to adapt and innovate. This means investing in our future, which is inextricably linked to investing in education. For instance, we must channel resources into technology and innovative teaching methods. We also need to ensure our students receive a comprehensive education, equipping them with the skills and knowledge essential to succeed in the global workforce.

Our educational systems must keep pace with rapid technological advancements and evolving economic landscapes. This will require financial investment and a commitment to fostering creativity, critical thinking, and adaptability in our students.

Many factors contribute to the failings of our education system, but the core issue stems from its antiquated roots. Our schooling system was conceived over two hundred years ago, designed for a world vastly different from ours. The skills currently emphasized in schools—such as conformity and obedience—no longer align with the demands of the modern economy. They often prove counterproductive.

Moreover, traditional schooling typically erodes students' innate curiosity and replaces it with a sense of indifference. This disengagement is one of the primary reasons why numerous individuals cease to pursue learning after leaving school, effectively stifling their unique voices and creativity. The repercussions of such an approach can be detrimental in the long run.

Compounding this issue, schools regularly propagate outdated information and biased narratives that can obstruct students' perceptions of the world. Consequently, many are ill-prepared for real-world challenges, handicapped by misconceptions ingrained during their schooling. It is disconcerting to consider that countless students graduate without the requisite skills or knowledge to thrive beyond academia.

To address these concerns, we need to reimagine our education system for the twenty-first century. This process begins with each of us assuming responsibility for our learning, fostering a culture of life-long curiosity and intellectual growth. By doing so, we can cultivate an educational environment that truly prepares students for the complexities and opportunities of the modern world.[17]

Education Flaws in the United States of America

The American education system shows signs of deterioration, failing to equip students with the skills required for real life. Consequently, college graduates struggle to find jobs, and those who do

---

[17]. Sunstrom, L., "School is for Fools: 10 Reasons the Education System is a Failure" 2019, (https://startgainingmomentum.com/school-fools-10-reasons-education-system-failure/).

often end up underemployed. The system cannot impart the necessary skills for success in the real world.

One potential remedy is greater parental involvement in their children's education. Parents should ensure their children complete their homework, attend school regularly, and strive for good grades.

Moreover, the government must commit more resources to education. It should guarantee that all schools have the necessary resources to provide quality education to every student. A glaring deficiency in the current system is a lack of emphasis on critical thinking, an indispensable skill that should be a cornerstone of education rather than mere rote learning.

Many schools are closing due to budget cuts and other financial constraints, signaling more profound issues within the system. The remaining schools struggle to deliver quality education due to these closures, depriving students of opportunities to succeed. Overworked and underpaid teachers, increasing class sizes, and declining educational quality are pressing issues that demand urgent attention.

The integration of technology into learning also warrants scrutiny. While it offers benefits, it also has drawbacks. Technology can enhance learning if used appropriately, but it can also serve as a distraction within the classroom. Furthermore, the cost of technology creates a barrier for some families, causing disparity in access to digital learning resources.

The lack of diversity in education hinders talented and brilliant students from reaching their full potential, an issue that demands immediate attention. Diversity fosters a sense of community and belonging, encouraging students to engage more in their education and take pride in their achievements.

Funding for education has stagnated or even declined in some states when adjusted for inflation. Underfunded schools struggle to provide necessary resources, hire qualified teachers, offer challenging coursework, or maintain infrastructure. As a result, students are deprived of the education they deserve.

This deficiency is evident in the lack of innovation in teacher education. Many teacher preparation programs have not evolved to meet the changing needs of schools and educators, leaving many teachers feeling ill-equipped to teach effectively in modern classrooms.

Furthermore, there is an overemphasis on standardized tests and accountability at the expense of teaching and learning. This focus diverts attention from encouraging critical thinking and learning and instead prepares students for tests.

The school-to-prison pipeline is a significant concern. Too many students are lost in this pipeline due to frequent suspensions or expulsions, leading to incarceration rather than receiving the needed help. Schools tend to punish students swiftly, even for minor offenses, instead of addressing the underlying issues. This approach exacerbates the problem, resulting in more suspensions and expulsions.

In the digital age, we must reassess our definition of literacy. Traditionally, literacy was confined to printed content. However, in our technology-driven society, literacy should encompass diverse media types, allowing students to engage with images, digital essays, and other formats beyond traditional paper books.

As we usher our children into adulthood, we must arm them with technical knowledge and skills pertinent to our digital era. A fundamental change in our educational approach is necessary to address this need. Instead of focusing predominantly on basic grammar rules, we should incorporate valuable lessons about computers and digital literacy into our curricula. This approach will ensure that children learn to read and write effectively and grasp the various facets of computer literacy.

Computer literacy comprises a set of skills enabling individuals to use computers efficiently. With technology's increasing prevalence, even a basic understanding of computer usage is essential for functioning effectively in personal and professional life. Critical aspects of computer literacy include navigating diverse software types, grasping fundamental computer programming, and utilizing various hardware. Additionally, those proficient in computer usage should employ the internet and other digital tools for research, communication, and collaboration.[18]

There are several avenues to gain computer literacy. Coding boot camps, for example, provide an intensive learning environment to grasp programming basics and diverse software usage. Tech giants like Microsoft and Apple offer courses about their products and other fundamental computer skills. Numerous online tutorials provide insights into computer basics and software usage. However, consistent practice is the most effective way to become computer literate. Frequent computer usage enhances proficiency for work, academic pursuits, or personal projects. Exploring new possibilities and pushing boundaries with computers can lead to remarkable skill improvement.

But why is universal access to computer literacy necessary? Various elements come into play when considering computer literacy. Some might view reading digital texts as a component, while others might see stringing together digital messages as part of communication literacy. Regardless, the demand for computer literacy skills is escalating. It is not solely about being able to use a computer; understanding its workings and troubleshooting abilities are equally vital.

The shortcomings in America's educational system cannot be attributed to a single issue. Instead, it is a confluence of challenges undermining the significance and fair distribution of quality education among learners from diverse backgrounds. Therefore, fostering computer literacy should be an integral part of our collective effort to address these challenges and equip future generations for success in the digital age.

The issues plaguing the United States education system are multifaceted, stemming from factors such as poverty rates, levels of minority participation, and parental involvement. For instance, in 2015,

---

18. Lynch, M., "20 Reasons Why the American Education System is Failing" The Tech Edvocate, 2021, (https://www.thetechedvocate.org/20-reasons-why-the-american-education-system-is-failing/).

a staggering $600 billion was spent annually on education in the US, but the most recent figures suggest a significant reduction to around $103 billion.[19,20]

There is a burgeoning interest in experiential learning, which equips students with practical skills that are increasingly relevant in today's technology-driven job market. However, shifting toward such an approach requires diverting funds from our current educational framework.

Despite an increased focus on education, there has been a concerning decline in the number of teachers. The teacher shortage in America's K-12 schools is a glaring issue. Enrollment in teacher preparation plans have been on a steady downward trajectory, with a 37.8 percent drop from the 2008–2009 cohort to the 2015–2016 graduates (27 percent).[21] This trend may be partially attributed to technological advancements, allowing for high-quality remote teaching and video streaming of classroom lectures. These innovations offer flexibility and potential cost savings.

Artificial intelligence not only enriches the learning experience for students but also liberates educators' time. They can then focus on the crux of their profession: teaching and guiding students on leveraging technology for self-education and exploring endless opportunities. One of the most glaring failures of traditional education systems is their struggle to keep pace with technological advancements. In a world where tablets could potentially replace textbooks, how can

---

[19]. Nelson, L., "America spends more than $600 billion on schools. Here's where it goes and why it matters" 2015, (https://www.vox.com/2015/3/25/8284637/school-spending-US).

[20]. Camera, L., "Biden's Budget Significantly Boosts K-12 Education Spending" 2021, (https://www.usnews.com/news/education-news/articles/2021-04-09/bidens-budget-significantly-boosts-k-12-education-spending).

[21]. García E. and Weiss E., "US schools struggle to hire and retain teachers. The second report in 'The Perfect Storm in the Teacher Labor Market' series" 2019, (https://www.epi.org/publication/u-s-schools-struggle-to-hire-and-retain-teachers-the-second-report-in-the-perfect-storm-in-the-teacher-labor-market-series/).

we expect educators unfamiliar with computers to effectively use technology in classrooms where all learning materials are digital?

Teachers should receive more training to enhance their current roles, aiding students in gaining knowledge from textbooks and external courses, online documentaries, and more. However, the conventional system struggles to adapt to the rapid advancement of technology and fails to cater to students with diverse learning styles. Furthermore, with a considerable number of teachers opting for early retirement, there is an increasing demand for new educators.

The question of how we can sustain our quality of life through education is thought-provoking and warrants further exploration. It is an invitation for introspection, challenging us to reimagine the role and delivery of education in our rapidly evolving society.

We must find innovative ways to integrate advancing technology into our education system. The most sophisticated AI algorithms can identify an uptick in disengaged students who struggle to thrive in school due to limited instructional time.

For instance, a study from the University of Michigan revealed that students spend more time engrossed in television or electronic devices (16.75 hours per week) than studying (4 hours per week).[22] This is a startling imbalance. Another study underscored that many teenagers devote up to thirty hours per week to "screen time."[23] While it may seem that teens are hopelessly addicted to their screens, there are ways we can redirect this tech affinity for educational purposes.

The American Heart Association has reported that most teenagers spend at least twenty hours per week watching TV or using computer monitors, with a sizable number clocking even more screen

---

[22]. "US children and teens spend more time on academics" (University Michigan Press, 2004, https://news.umich.edu/u-s-children-and-teens-spend-more-time-on-academics/).

[23]. American Heart Association, "Many Teens Spend 30 Hours A Week On 'Screen Time' During High School" 2008, (https://www.sciencedaily.com/releases/2008/03/080312172614.htm).

time.[24,25] This hitherto recreational screen time could be transformed into a learning opportunity with the judicious use of educational technology.

AI offers a promising solution to accommodate the ever-increasing student population. However, a caveat exists. The declining number of teachers presents challenges, such as the inability to provide the hands-on education students may require. There is a delicate balance between leveraging technology for efficiency and maintaining the human touch that nurtures a stimulating learning environment.

Foundation models in education

The traditional school model, reminiscent of a factory production line, is ill-suited to catering to the diverse needs of twenty-first-century students. We must shift toward an education model that prioritizes the individual learner and their unique requirements. This chapter will delve into three foundational models in education designed to tailor a more personalized learning experience for students.

The first model under discussion is the modular model, which dissects a task into smaller, manageable parts, allowing students to progress at their own pace. This approach proves beneficial for students who learn differently or struggle with test-taking. The second model, project-based learning, enables students to apply learned concepts to real-world scenarios. This participatory approach resonates with learners who prefer experiential learning. Lastly, the competency-based model allows students to advance based on their mastery of skills and concepts, favoring those who require additional time to absorb information or struggle with exams.

---

24. McCormick, Alexander C., It's About Time: What to Make of Reported Declines in How Much College Students Study Association of American Colleges & Universities Liberal Education, (Win 2011, https://www.aacu.org/publications-research/periodicals/its-about-time-what-make-reported-declines-how-much-college), v97 n1 p30–39.
25. Welch, A., "Health experts say parents need to drastically cut kids' screen time" CBS News, 2018, (https://www.cbsnews.com/news/parents-need-to-drastically-cut-kids-screen-time-devices-american-heart-association/).

While each model has its merits, it falls on educators to discern which best suits their students' needs. However, it is crucial to understand that no single model is flawless. Educators should remain open to adapting their teaching methodologies according to their students' evolving needs.

Foundation models are complex and dynamic systems used to simulate real-world conditions. They share a critical trait—self-supervision.[26] The term "foundation" might lack a technical definition, but it can be applied when an agent's behavior evolves after interacting with its environment. This adaptability allows these models to be a basis for reasoning about their fundamental properties, adjusting over time as new research emerges. Examples include reinforcement learning, where an agent learns to behave in a specific environment by receiving rewards for successful choices, and evolution, where agents (organisms) adapt over time to suit their environment better.

This adaptability is pivotal, as it enables foundation models to stay abreast of new research and environmental changes. In the ever-evolving education landscape, these models can incorporate the latest research findings, ensuring they remain current. Moreover, they can help create a more personalized learning experience for students.

Foundation models are already driving educational transformations. Examples include using MathBERT for "knowledge tracing" and algorithms that interpret students' answers generated from personal understanding, such as coding questions or sentences extracted from prior readings. Furthermore, foundation models aid students in developing intuition about physical systems that can later be studied in greater detail.

A significant challenge in providing student feedback is the limited understanding of AI models. For instance, if there were an error with code or physics problems, students would not know how to proceed due to the lack of data. To offer effective feedback, two essential

---

26. Rishi Bommasani, Drew A. Hudson, E., On the Opportunities and Risks of Foundation Models. Center for Research on Foundation Models (CRFM), (Cornell University Press, 2021).

capabilities are required: a thorough comprehension of the material and the diagnostic skills necessary to assess each task. Current AI models lack these skills, especially when faced with the vast data generated in typical classrooms or online courses.

Herein lies the value of foundation models. They can learn from minimal data and understand the course content, allowing them to provide tailored student feedback. In other words, foundation models can diagnose students' mistakes and provide feedback that helps them improve. The demand for better systems stems from the desire to provide a quality education that captures the complex reasoning behind each action.

Envision a foundation model adept at solving mathematical problems, but the challenge lies in creating one that can diagnose and rectify misconceptions based on students' responses. To tackle this issue, I propose a different approach to providing feedback. Instead of giving explicit instructions on areas requiring improvement, we should offer guidance for students working on open-ended tasks like writing short paragraphs or drawing diagrams. Direct instructions may inadvertently stifle critical thinking, while our goal is to foster creativity and challenge constraints without imposing rigid demands. We aim to make the "productive struggle" more tangible, enabling students to reflect on their work with enriched insight.

In achieving this, we must first focus on developing models capable of recognizing resilience in students, identifying those who are grappling with challenges but not surrendering. Concurrently, we need models that can capture signs of student engagement and discern when a student's response, though correct, is not optimal, signaling growth opportunities. It is vital to consider the diverse learning needs of students, considering their varying stages of development and unique learning trajectories.

For instance, a foundation model might effectively assist a student struggling with a math problem, but it may fall short when aiding a student wrestling with paragraph construction. Each foundation model has its strengths and weaknesses, making it imperative to identify the most suitable one for each student.

Ultimately, with an appropriate foundation model, we can inspire students to think critically and creatively, challenging them to unlock their full potential. In essence, foundation models are indispensable educational tools, serving as catalysts that facilitate students' continuous learning and evolution.

Education with artificial intelligence

Artificial intelligence is far from a recent phenomenon, and many of us already interact with its systems in some form. There are countless ways AI can revolutionize education, making learning more engaging for students worldwide, and not all involve tangible technology like robots. This groundbreaking frontier could be conducted in an era where individuals have more time for activities beyond constant learning at work.

Education is a fundamental pillar of our society, influencing all aspects of life, from healthcare to entrepreneurship. It shapes our worldview and self-perception. Thus, the critical question is: how will AI-modified teaching impact society? Given that its physical manifestation is intangible, its potential influence should not be underestimated. It can alter our interaction with information, potentially bridging the digital divide between those without access to digital resources.

Evidence of AI's impact on education is emerging. Will it render teachers obsolete, or will it create jobs in programming and maintaining these machines? Furthermore, it may change how students learn. AI holds immense potential within the educational context. One aspect of AI that disrupts education is its ability to automate teachers' tasks and duties. This can be viewed as a boon or bane, depending on perspective. Automating teaching could increase participation and lead to higher-paying jobs. However, if automation replaces teachers, fewer jobs will be available in education, potentially exacerbating unemployment rates.

Nevertheless, AI assuming more tasks previously undertaken by educators affords teachers more time to focus on other facets of education. For instance, AI could revolutionize educational systems through automated grading. As more students enroll in advanced classes and achieve better grades, traditional grading methods may become obsolete. Algorithm-based grading is just one way AI is transforming education.

Another facet of AI that impacts education is personalized learning plans tailored to each student's unique needs. Teachers could utilize AI-generated lesson plans, allowing all students to succeed. Personalized, interactive lessons with customized commentary can support students requiring extra help, addressing prevalent concerns like bullying and a lack of motivation among students.

The advent of technology that merges education, entertainment, and games has made learning more engaging than ever. It has sparked interest in STEM fields among high school students worldwide and can potentially make education highly personalized. Instead of a one-size-fits-all approach, education could focus on a student's strengths and areas requiring improvement. Schools would have access to unbiased student data, enabling targeted instruction.

The next generation of learners may never experience a knowledge deficit if they are willing to learn and stay informed. This is evident in recent technological advancements like Content Technologies' AI-driven digital platforms, which offer learning challenges for prekindergarten through college levels. AI tools targeted at K–12 education markets track progress over time, allowing educators to intervene before problems escalate.

Students receiving personalized feedback are more likely to strengthen their skills. AI will transform education by providing real-time insights into students' progress, saving educators hours of document review or repetitive teaching approaches. Advanced chatbots can support educational programs by answering complex questions and monitoring students' comprehension. However, over-reliance on such systems could hinder children's development of essential life skills.

While chatbots may not entirely replace teachers, they have the potential to enhance teaching efficacy and efficiency significantly. These intelligent systems can clarify complex queries, review students' reading material, and monitor comprehension levels. However, overreliance on advanced chatbots could inadvertently foster dependency on even rudimentary tasks like scheduling appointments or purchasing groceries. This could challenge children learning to accomplish these tasks independently as they become accustomed to depending on chatbots instead.

Concerns about AI's application in education have been voiced alongside these benefits. If improperly implemented, AI could lead to unintended negative consequences, such as impeding a student's access to education or disseminating inaccurate information. Therefore, it is crucial for educators not only to instruct students about the potential benefits of this emerging technology for their future careers but also to equip them with the knowledge to safeguard against potential risks.

AI's integration into schools is not without drawbacks. As robots assume more roles traditionally performed by humans, there could be a decrease in human workforce involvement. This shift could potentially affect children's education negatively. For instance, it could result in fewer children desiring to learn from human teachers with practical, firsthand knowledge of topics unique to human experiences, such as learning resilience to overcome obstacles or cultivating creativity by exploring unconventional solutions.

Regardless, it is undeniable that AI will disrupt education—it is a matter of when, not if. Hence, the earlier educators integrate this technology into their classrooms, the more beneficial it will be for current and future generations. By balancing and leveraging AI's advantages and mitigating its risks, we can create an enriching educational landscape that prepares students for the future while preserving the irreplaceable human element in education.

How artificial intelligence can transform education

Countries worldwide embrace artificial intelligence integration into their educational systems. Given its transformative impact on data processing, storage, and decision-making, extending AI's influence on learning is logical.

Innovative technologies like virtual reality offer a fresh approach for students keen on exploring novel topics or delving into subjects outside their usual purview. These tools can render complex concepts more digestible by dissecting them into smaller, manageable segments. These technologies can enhance comprehension by offering a unique perspective and simplifying learning. Artificial intelligence can provide specific feedback to help improve skills ranging from reading comprehension to musical instrument proficiency. This personalized learning experience tailored to each student's needs may prove more effective than traditional teaching methods.

As AI continues to evolve at a breakneck pace, it will invariably alter our interaction with technology. One of our foremost responsibilities is understanding how AI can assist us and its implications for education. As AI becomes increasingly sophisticated, researchers are finding innovative ways to harness these advancements in niches like education. For instance, an app called ActiveLearn[27] employs machine-learning algorithms developed at MIT Media Lab to customize lessons based on individual students' needs.

However, businesses were initially unprepared for an AI-driven future. According to Servion Global Solutions, by 2025, intelligent machines will drive 95 percent of customer interactions, including live

---

[27]. ActiveLearn, 2021, (https://www.pearsonactivelearn.com/app/Home).

telephone conversations and online chats.[28] The emphasis has shifted toward equipping children with the skills to interact with computers rather than traditional learning methods like reading from books or studying maps on globes. AI in education could manifest through personal assistants such as Siri or Alexa,[29] providing a supportive platform for student learning.

One notable example is the intelligent tutoring system (ITS), which utilizes an intelligent agent (AI) to automate the teaching process, delivering subjects like math or physics more efficiently than humans alone. Established in 1977, this company's adaptive learning engine and over a million student users recently experienced significant success. It considers a student's prior knowledge and adapts the course content based on their responses.

The benefits of using AI in education are manifold, including increased accuracy and efficiency, substantial time savings for teachers, and enhanced student motivation. Despite the uncertainties of our era, AI has emerged as a formidable ally in navigating educational reform. It offers personalized support and a wealth of resources, poised to revolutionize how we learn.

The future computer will not merely be a device but also a personal tutor, drawing on infinite data sets from internet searches to scientific journals and delivering tailored, relevant, and automatically updated lessons.

AI education without human interaction

The future of education, intertwined with the advancement of AI, remains shrouded in uncertainty. If technological progression continues at its current exponential rate, we could foresee a seismic shift in learning methods, potentially eliminating the need for human

---

28. "AI Will Power 95% Of Customer Interactions By 2025" Finance Digest Press (https://www.financedigest.com/ai-will-power-95-of-customer-interactions-by-2025.html).

29. Amazon Web Services, Inc., 2021, Alexa in Education (https://aws.amazon.com/education/alexa-edu/).

interaction. However, even if AI's growth does not accelerate exponentially, questions persist about whether society is ready to replace human educators with what some perceive as emotionless, pre-programmed machines.

The most critical aspect to consider when envisioning AI's role in education is the impact these interactions will have on the learning process. As AI evolves, we are inching closer to an educational landscape that operates independently of human intervention. The implications of this transformation remain unclear, raising numerous questions about our future and how we can aptly prepare for it.

Imagine an educational environment devoid of teachers or students, where an AI system adapts to and learns from individuals and vice versa. We are already seeing the initial phases of this evolution, with robots guiding people through various tasks. However, these robots are not operating autonomously—they need human guidance to learn from interactions with AI.

This concept has been a staple of science fiction narratives, often depicting worlds ruled by robots and AI systems that vie for control over humanity's future. A fascinating question arises from these narratives: should these machines serve or replace us entirely? One certainty remains—technology alone cannot resolve all of humanity's challenges. It demands the integration of valuable, preexisting social skills to continue thriving.

One of humanity's greatest strengths is our capacity to learn from others and transmit knowledge across generations. This characteristic emphasizes the need for humans to devise strategies for our species to continue thriving, rather than letting machines programmed solely for predetermined tasks replace us. Despite the rapid advancements in AI, the quintessential human ability to think critically, adapt, and innovate remains irreplaceable.

Augmented reality (AR)

Since 2013, teachers have been utilizing augmented reality (AR) as an innovative educational tool.[30] As we dedicate more time and resources to knowledge acquisition, the necessity for innovation becomes apparent. This implies a transformation in our teaching methodologies, integrating emerging technologies into the educational landscape. With the evolution of augmented reality over the years, it can now effectively elucidate complex concepts in the classroom.

One potential application involves the use of smart glasses equipped with AR capabilities. Students could follow animated instructions to conduct experiments or solve problems, interacting with virtual characters and objects within their physical environment. For instance, arrows could point to specific areas of interest, enhancing their understanding.

This avant-garde approach allows teachers more opportunities for individual interactions with students while fostering creativity through problem-solving strategies gleaned from real-world scenarios and software simulations. Educators are actively transitioning from traditional lecturing to more engaging teaching methods, as demonstrated by innovative game-based learning platforms like Kahoot!.[31] However, our responsibility remains to ensure fair access to education for all students. Kahoot!'s system enables teachers to assess student comprehension and engagement in classroom learning swiftly. Students answer questions on mobile devices as part of a global competition challenge, facilitating learning anytime, anywhere.

In a world where technology permeates nearly every facet of our lives, opinions vary on its educational implications. Some perceive an impending robotic takeover of teaching roles, while others expect a new, personalized, practical education era. Challenges will inevitably

---

[30]. Quintero, J., Baldiris, S., Rubira, R., Cerón J. & Velez, G., "Augmented Reality in Educational Inclusion. A Systematic Review on the Last" Frontiers in Psychology Decade, 2019, (https:// doi: 10.3389/fpsyg.2019.01835).

[31]. Kahoot.com, 2021, (https://kahoot.com/).

arise as AI becomes increasingly prevalent, opening boundless opportunities for innovative learning.

Challenges may include a heightened need for teachers to be technologically adept and the possibility of students becoming overly dependent on AI tutors. However, the rise of AI also presents numerous opportunities for pedagogical innovation. For instance, AI can facilitate the creation of interactive, engaging lessons. Instead of relying solely on textbook material, teachers could utilize AI programs to orchestrate multimedia classes incorporating videos, quizzes, and other interactive elements. This makes lessons more engaging for students and bolsters their learning efficacy.

How AI can improve education with augmented reality and machine learning algorithms

The prospect of a wiser world is increasingly tangible, particularly with recent artificial intelligence advancements. AI has made significant strides in areas like deep learning and object detection in computer vision. However, unchecked progress could make our "imperfect" human minds obsolete, as machines—needing no sleep, socialization, or sustenance—outperform us.

A key aspect to consider here is machine learning, a subset of AI that uses data to learn independently. When new information is added, the system learns from it without requiring specific pre-programming. This capability can lead to the creation of robots that perform tasks without human intervention, disrupting traditional educational methods. Education is evolving from merely transmitting knowledge to facilitating students learning how to learn. This shift could transform schools into experimentation hubs, liberating teachers from instruction and allowing them to work closely with individual students, ensuring concept mastery and comprehension of underlying principles.

Imagine harnessing the power of augmented reality in education. It superimposes interactive 3D graphics and real-time data onto real-world objects or scenarios. The potential for educational innovation through AR is boundless. It offers users a depth of understanding beyond what traditional books can provide. The advantages of integrating AR into learning include faster comprehension rates, an over 400 percent improvement in retention rate, and enhanced understanding due to visual cues and audio feedback.

Integrating augmented reality into educational settings offers students a unique learning experience, blending visual representations with auditory cues. Owing to its interactive nature, AR enriches educational content through guided, step-by-step tutorials within realistic environments. This immersive experience allows students to explore and manipulate their surroundings, effectively bridging the gap between theoretical knowledge and practical experience—a critical function of education.

The introduction of AR into classrooms has been shown to improve student engagement, reducing distractions and boredom due to the immersive nature of the content. Consequently, teachers and students report higher satisfaction levels with the learning experience.

Augmented reality holds considerable promise as an educational tool, potentially enhancing student retention rates and better preparing them for future careers. One of its most significant advantages is the capacity for personalized learning.[32] It can tailor lessons to each student's needs, creating a more inclusive and effective learning environment. This personalization makes each student feel prioritized when interacting with AR technology in the classroom.

Recent advancements in AR technology have unlocked new possibilities for educators worldwide. By overlaying virtual data onto real-world objects or scenarios using mobile devices or computers, it

---

[32]. Papanastasiou, G.P., Drigas, A., Skianis, C. and Lytras M., "Virtual and augmented reality effects on K-12, higher and tertiary education students' twenty-first-century skills" (https:// doi:10.1007/s10055-018-0363-2).

allows students to partake in complex or otherwise unfeasible activities.[33] This innovative approach fosters a more in-depth understanding of various subjects and enhances the learning experience. As AR continues to evolve, its role in education is expected to expand, providing even more immersive, personalized learning opportunities.

Augmented reality allows educators to create novel and engaging learning opportunities for their students. For instance, students no longer need access to traditional school facilities like science labs equipped with expensive apparatus such as microscopes. Now, they can have similar experiences right from their homes. It provides an interactive learning experience that traditional teaching methods may not offer across subjects like math, science, history, or literature.

This revolution in education has spurred a global movement among educators and entrepreneurs, aiming to devise innovative ways for students, teachers, parents, and society at large to benefit from AR education. Predictions indicate that by 2024, over one billion people will use augmented reality regularly, marking a significant shift toward AR in education.[34]

The next phase of AR in education involves further testing and evaluating its impact on students and teachers. Research has shown that students who used AR could recall more details and concepts and were more engaged in learning than those who relied on traditional methods like reading textbooks or attending lectures.

Augmented reality tools, currently accessible primarily in school settings, are expected to be available for home use soon. These tools overlay additional information onto a subject's reality, projecting images from digital cameras onto surfaces like desks or tables and transforming them into interactive screens controlled by hand gestures and voice commands.

---

[33]. "Augmented reality in education: teaching tool or passing trend" *The Guardian* Press, 2013, (https://www.theguardian.com/higher-education-network/blog/2013/feb/11/augmented-reality-teaching-tool-trend).

[34]. Alsop, T., "Global mobile augmented reality (AR) users 2024" Statista, 2021, (https://www.statista.com/statistics/1098630/global-mobile-augmented-reality-ar-users/).

Its efficiency spans various domains, including mathematics, physics, and geometry, in K–12 curricula and higher education. It offers students immersive experiences and stimulates their curiosity, enabling them to explore new worlds virtually without prior knowledge.[35]

AR's potential for educational innovation lies in its ability to make concepts more narrative, interactive, and tangible through the visual representation of data or geographic locations otherwise inaccessible. Imagine using your phone or tablet as a gateway to new realms of knowledge and discovery.

Schools have leveraged AR technology to provide immersive learning experiences for students who might otherwise not have that opportunity due to budget constraints or physical limitations, including autism spectrum disorder and intellectual disabilities. It has also introduced a new way for teachers and students to learn about ancient cultures through games like Rome Reborn VR, bridging the gap between the past and the present in an immersive and engaging way.[36]

Advantages and disadvantages of education with AI

AI has been a concept since the 1950s, but it has gained substantial traction recently due to developments in machine learning and big data.[37] These advancements have enabled AI to tackle more complex tasks, suggesting that AI's role in education will significantly change in the coming years.

However, the benefits of AI are a topic of debate. Despite its potential, certain aspects necessitate human input, such as teaching children. A potential downside of AI in education is the risk of privacy

35. Papanastasiou, G.P., Drigas, A., Skianis, C., and Lytras M., "Virtual and augmented reality effects on K-12, higher and tertiary education students' twenty-first-century skills" (https://doi:10.1007/s10055-018-0363-2).

36. Romereborn.org, 2021, (https://www.romereborn.org/).

37. Bentley, P., "What is artificial intelligence?" *BBC Science Focus Magazine*, 2020, (https://www.sciencefocus.com/future-technology/artificial-intelligence-ai/?msclkid=2250883da7601lecaecbb1a9a157b6be).

breaches and infringements on students' rights. To function effectively, AI requires high-quality, consistent datasets, the collection of which can sometimes be intrusive.

Nevertheless, the benefits of this technology are immense. It can free up teachers' time to focus on students who require additional assistance, potentially reducing class sizes by half. Artificial intelligence can analyze student data and adjust coursework accordingly, personalizing instruction to each student's needs and abilities. This personalized approach can improve performance and grades, helping students learn more effectively. It benefits students who learn best through visual or auditory stimuli. Over time, these AI programs become more adaptable, reducing the need for instructor intervention. It also extends access to high-quality, engaging educational content to regions where traditional education may be hindered due to safety or economic issues. The ability for students to learn at their own pace and anywhere offers unprecedented freedom.

This technology allows students more time to explore their passions, interests, and hobbies with instant feedback. Teachers can guide students toward career paths that align with their interests, benefiting both students and society. The advent of AI in education addresses significant challenges students face, especially in high school and college.

Higher education institutions should not underestimate the impact of AI. This technology can enhance students' understanding and mastery of the material, leading to higher retention rates and less time wasted in introductory courses. AI can customize curricula based on student progress, eliminating unnecessary repetition of known concepts. Moreover, students can collaborate on their studies and receive help from tutors globally, highlighting the potential of AI-based education to revolutionize learning. AI can also ease the financial burden of education. It can reduce tuition fees by providing competent, adaptive learning opportunities as nonphysical entities. This solution ensures students can learn in a secure environment without straining their budget, instilling confidence in parents that their children receive quality instruction at home. The future of learning is empowering, adaptive, and globally accessible. Thanks to AI.

While AI holds immense potential for transforming education, it is essential to acknowledge its challenges. One such challenge is the difficulty consumers may face in understanding the benefits of AI in education. This could increase inequality, as adopting AI-enabled technologies might create entry barriers for those without high-speed internet or advanced technologies.

However, it is essential to recognize how beneficial AI can be for children in developing countries who lack access to high-quality public schools or even crucial educational resources. Studies have shown that providing underprivileged students access to top-quality educational resources via computer screens can improve their performance to match, if not surpass, that of their peers in wealthier countries.

Innovative minds are exploring the potential of AI to offer all children, regardless of their location or socioeconomic status, the best possible learning opportunities. For instance, some schools in the United States are taking a creative approach to their educational systems by implementing AI.[38] They use robots as teaching assistants for subjects like math and science, offering students an engaging and efficient learning experience.[39]

While AI has educational disadvantages, focusing on turning these challenges into opportunities is crucial. For example, incorporating AI into teaching math or science requires students to understand how machines think and solve problems, a skill not typically in-

---

38. Sears, K., "STEM Education Innovation Lab Partners with Gwinnett County Schools to Offer Innovative AgSTEM Learning Experience" 2020, (https://den.mercer.edu/stem-education-innovation-lab-partners-with-gwinnett-county-schools-to-offer-innovative-agstem-learning-experience/?msclkid=16ad6606a7611eca5d5f1a01c26ceb8).

39. Luna, H., "How AI will Completely Transform Education" Digital Trends, 2017, (https://blogs.csun.edu/aix/2017/09/28/how-ai-will-completely-transform-education-digital-trends/?msclkid=759e3ff6a7a911eca1d2b68b773d84f3).

cluded in current curricula. However, this can be viewed as an opportunity rather than a disadvantage. Education's primary goal is to prepare children for the future, and understanding AI—an increasingly integral part of our world—is a crucial component of that preparation. Thus, its advantages in education can significantly outweigh the alternatives, providing a more inclusive and effective global educational landscape for differently abled individuals.

CHAPTER 3

Types of Interactions

Artificial intelligence is indeed revolutionizing both teaching and learning. It enables more personalized, adaptive, and dynamic educational experiences for students while freeing up teachers to focus on creating engaging and creative lessons. As technology enters every aspect of our lives, AI's integration into education is inevitable.

Artificial intelligence is not just about tailoring educational content to individual students but also about reshaping the role of educators. Teachers are no longer just providers of pre-made content; they are facilitators, guiding students to create their own knowledge. It can assist teachers in crafting exciting lessons that cater to each student's unique needs while connecting them to relevant educational resources through personalized learning plans. This does not imply that robots will replace teachers; instead, it underscores the value of human creativity and educational insight.

However, realizing the transformative potential of AI in education requires the right resources and tools. We need to shift our perspective and stop viewing AI as a threat to education but as a tool designed to enhance our effectiveness. AI offers numerous opportunities to improve educational practices, from designing inclusive assessments for differently abled students to creating more efficient tracking of student progress.

In an AI-powered educational landscape, we must rethink our understanding of pedagogy. Traditional teaching, where the educator controls the learning process, must evolve into a more student-centric approach. In AI-powered classrooms, students have more outstanding agency over their learning, dictating what and how they want to learn. This shift necessitates educators who can facilitate learning rather than dictate it.

This new form of pedagogy focuses on adapting to the learner's needs and helping them learn in a way that suits them best. It involves understanding how different students learn and using that information to craft a tailored learning experience for each one. Undoubtedly, this is a significant shift in classroom dynamics, but it promises to be a more effective teaching method in the long run.

Howard Gardner's theory of multiple intelligences provides a valuable framework for understanding how AI might impact a range of learners. For instance, linguistic learners might benefit from AI systems emphasizing reading and writing, while logical learners might thrive with AI tools that work with numbers and patterns. By understanding how students with various learning styles absorb information, artificial intelligence can help design personalized learning experiences tailored to their individual needs, leading to a more efficient and effective education system that caters to all learners.

Teachers' interactions with AI

Artificial intelligence in education has the potential to revolutionize teaching and learning, offering profound benefits for both teachers and students. One of AI's most significant advantages is its capacity to respond to questions that students might find difficult or misunderstand—a task that has traditionally been the responsibility of teachers.

The overarching goal of implementing AI in classrooms is to leverage technological advancements to facilitate a more personalized, individualized approach to teaching. Teachers can use AI tools to monitor student progress during class sessions and homework assignments, increasing engagement and improving academic performance.

Artificial intelligence can particularly benefit at-risk students or those struggling academically due to mental health conditions such as attention deficit disorder (ADD) or depression. These conditions often go unnoticed until students start to lag in their academics. Schools can use AI to identify and address these issues early on, creating a more supportive learning environment. It can also help cross-reference non-academic factors that impact a student's education, such as family conflicts or peer bullying. For example, Amazon's Alexa for Education (A4E)[40] is an AI-powered program that teaches interactions through voice commands on devices like Echo Dot.[41,42]

The coursework and assessments throughout the year help create personalized curricula for students at all levels of learning. It could be especially beneficial to low-income or minority children, who often lack the resources to accommodate their needs and make schooling more engaging and effective.

Teachers can use AI to guide students through their lessons, asking questions that provide real-time feedback. Many teachers have reported that real-time feedback makes teaching easier and improves student engagement and performance without increasing costs.

The goal of AI in education is to develop and deliver personalized instruction that makes learning more engaging and interactive. This approach allows students to leverage their strengths, develop new skills, and prepare for their future careers while ensuring they keep pace with rapidly evolving fields. AI in education is not just about technology; it is about using technology to empower students and educators.

Artificial intelligence is reshaping the educational landscape, making it easier for remote educators, such as online tutors. With an in-

---

[40]. Hudson, H., "20 Educational Games and Activities for Alexa" 2020, (https://www.weareteachers.com/educational-alexa-skills/?mscl-kid=1f34ec5da7aa11ecba6f1f039a07aa7e).

[41]. Business Insider. "'What is the Amazon Echo Dot?': Everything you need to know about Amazon's compact smart speaker" 2021, (https://www.businessinsider.com/what-is-amazon-echo-dot).

[42]. Greenwald D.,2023, "Amazon Echo Dot (5th Gen, 2022 Release) Review, https://www.pcmag.com/reviews/amazon-echo-dot-5th-gen

ternet connection, it eliminates travel time for lesson planning and offers a more efficient way to teach and learn. AI-powered technology can supplement and even replace human interactions, allowing teaching remotely through AI software that mimics a human tutor in video chat programs like Google Hangouts or Skype.[43,44] This advancement allows personalized instruction and saves time and money by eliminating travel expenses.

A significant aspect of AI is its potential to make education more inclusive. Artificial intelligence can create systems that understand complex instructions and hold meaningful conversations, enhancing the learning experience. Studies have shown that virtual environments like Second Life and Active Worlds can significantly boost student engagement.[45] These platforms offer increased interaction and community-building opportunities, reducing feelings of isolation and dropout rates. Users represent themselves with avatars from a list or created through a simple prototype, allowing them a greater sense of social presence than if they had not done so.[46]

One of the primary sources of anxiety for many individuals is the uncertainty encountered during interactions with others. Using AI technology to teach relational skills has emerged as a significant boon, empowering users with greater control and confidence when engaging in social interactions.

Teaching children with autism, for instance, presents a unique set of challenges.[47] These children often struggle with interpreting facial expressions and social cues, leading to a preference for isolation from

---

[43]. Skype.com. 2021, (https://www.skype.com/en/).

[44]. Hangouts.google.com. 2021, (https://hangouts.google.com/).

[45]. Smith-Robbins, S. "Higher Education as Virtual Conversation" EDUCAUSE Review, vol. 43, no. 5, 2008, (https://er.educause.edu/articles/2008/9/higher-education-as-virtual-conversation?msclkid=cde9392da82b11eca4cf34cc2f1016bb).

[46]. Wallace, P. and Marryott, J., "The impact of avatar self-representation on collaboration in virtual worlds" *Journal of Online Education*, 5 (5), 2009, (1–6).

[47]. Holz, S., "How AI is changing special education" 2017, (https://blog.neolms.com/ai-changing-special-education/).

their peers during school hours and outside the classroom.[48,49] This difficulty in social integration can further exacerbate their anxiety and disconnect.

Recognizing this issue, some educational institutions have turned to AI as a part of their strategy to enhance social interaction skills. These AI-driven tools are designed to improve crucial interpersonal skills in students who may otherwise struggle without additional support.[50] By leveraging AI's capabilities, schools aim to create a more inclusive and nurturing learning environment for all students, particularly those on the autism spectrum.

For a child with autism, AI glasses are like having an extra set of eyes.[51] The cameras on these frames help them read facial emotions and know how best to act in different situations. Researchers at Stanford University created it to assist children who struggle with reading social cues from people around them or identifying emotions conveyed by certain expressions when interacting with others face-to-face (known as mild cognitive impairment). This helps make life easier and more fulfilling due to its ability to assist without judgment. The glasses are attached to a smartphone app that uses machine learning algorithms to read facial emotions. The built-in camera takes photos of the wearer's surroundings, processes these images, and then sends instructions to the glasses, telling them how best to present themselves.

---

[48]. Artificial Intelligence Research, "Neural Network Shows People with Autism Read Expressions Differently" Tohoku University, 2021, (https://www.onartificialintelligence.com/articles/24463/neural-network-shows-people-with-autism-read-expressions-differently).

[49]. "AI glasses help children with autism read facial expressions" Springwise, 2016, (https://www.springwise.com/ai-glasses-helps-children-autism-read-facial-expressions/).

[50]. Solomon, O., "The uses of technology for and with children with Autism Spectrum Disorders" 2012, (https://www.researchgate.net/publication/281067142_The_uses_of_technology_for_and_with_children_with_Autism_Spectrum_Disorders).

[51]. Design Indaba, "Smart glasses help kids with autism recognize facial expressions and emotions" 2018, Retrieved from (https://anotherlightup.designindaba.com/articles/creative-work/smart-glasses-help-kids-autism-recognise-facial-expressions-and-emotions?msclkid=6301fd30a7ad11ecb2b5a3dd03bfcaa8).

Innovation in testing and assessment

In today's rapidly evolving world, innovations are emerging at an unprecedented pace. This is true in education, where innovative solutions and novel approaches to measuring student learning outcomes are regularly introduced. However, with these swift changes, it can be challenging for educators to stay abreast of the latest developments.

One such innovation that is gaining traction in some educational settings is weighted testing. This approach involves assessing students using unique prompts and questions, which fosters greater creativity and enhances learning outcomes. Weighted tests create a more enriching experience for teachers and students and actively involve students in their learning process.

Weighted tests also serve as a tool for AI to engage with students in novel ways, helping them learn about their assets and weaknesses. This understanding aids in molding them into successful adults. The rationale behind weighted tests is their inclusion of tasks requiring diverse skill sets, such as drawing or manipulating objects. These assessments aim to educate young people beyond the confines of textbooks and classrooms. By engaging students directly in practical tasks, we prepare them for the real-world challenges they will encounter when they step into society. Thus, weighted tests represent a significant step toward a more holistic, relevant, and engaging education.

Personalized instruction

In the past, learning was often confined to reading a single book. Today, one can delve into multiple books on assorted topics with AI-assisted virtual tutoring. The future of education will undoubtedly harness AI to serve students better. Imagine a world where children are recognized as unique individuals, receiving personalized instruction tailored to their strengths, weaknesses, and aspirations. Hasn't the idea of individualized education always been desirable? With AI technology, it is now within reach!

Artificial intelligence facilitates enhanced engagement and comprehension because the instruction is tailored for each student. With more accurate assessments of a student's needs, teachers can individualize their lessons for each pupil. In this system, an AI tutor delivers a student-centric curriculum that adapts to each student's learning style, ensuring no student is left behind. This vision of the future of education is exciting and promising.

Several AI-based startups have emerged, offering students a personalized educational experience while aiding teachers in managing their workload effectively. For instance, Querium, an educational platform, provides customizable STEM tutoring lessons for high school and college students. It analyzes answers, the time taken to complete sessions, and strengths across various topics.[52] This data equips teachers with insights into a student's learning habits and highlights areas for improvement.

Such platforms ensure that students can access current information, reducing the time teachers need to update lesson materials. Querium exemplifies how AI is disrupting the traditional education model with an effective, efficient, and innovative approach, enhancing the learning experience for students, and freeing up time for educators.[53]

Furthermore, software called Century Tech aids teachers in identifying potential issues in a student's learning style or content knowledge.[54] This tool has significantly improved students' grades compared to those without such assistance. Using machine learning algorithms, educators can tailor lesson plans for individual students based on their needs and interests. This approach ensures that every student receives instruction explicitly tailored to their learning requirements in each lesson. However, the impact of AI goes beyond individual customization. The studies themselves can undergo dramatic transformations based on AI's input. This could mean adapting the

---

[52]. Querium (http://querium.com/).

[53]. Schroer, A., "AI In Education: 12 Companies You Should Know" 2018, Updated 2022, (https://builtin.com/artificial-intelligence/ai-in-education).

[54]. CENTURY English, Maths, and Science, 2022, (https://www.century.tech/?mscl-kid=07ced7e9a7b211eca2febeb346a855fc).

content, style, or pace of instruction to optimize student engagement and comprehension.

Another technology disrupting education is AI Educator, which uses an artificial intelligence algorithm that analyzes a student's performance over time and identifies what skills are needed.[55] It then provides personalized learning content in areas with some potential weaknesses so that educators can provide targeted lessons with individualized teaching plans. The AI Educator system provides personalized feedback by analyzing student progress and reviewing past activities and goals achieved in previous work sessions. Finally, it matches this information with instructional strategies that target specific skill gaps, thus providing schools with a path to one-size-fits-all, relevant when dealing with students' individuality or talents.

Students can navigate through a personalized dashboard to find the content they are looking for. With just a click, they can track progress, identify areas of mastery or weakness, and access required lessons. Emerging technologies like AI-powered tools that personalize learning experiences, predict student success rates, or recommend supplemental classes are increasingly prevalent in schools.

These innovations have improved grades among those who use them consistently. For example, AI computers can now give students a much more incredible opportunity for academic success than peers who do not receive this extra attention from technology or do not have adequate school information.

The potential of AI in education transcends classroom instruction. It could include programming AI with skills applicable in real-world work environments, allowing students to practice these skills safely. Furthermore, AI can monitor the effectiveness of our education system by evaluating vast amounts of data to detect patterns that might indicate potential problems in educating today's students, thereby uncovering ways to enhance it. It is not just an educational tool; it is a

---

[55]. Aieducator.2021, (https://aieducator.com/).

pathway to a more personalized, practical, and forward-thinking learning experience.

Artificial intelligence has tremendous potential for enhancing learning experiences and offering unique formal and informal education opportunities. For instance, it can provide teachers with insightful data about students' progress in their home studies, thereby enabling more effective, individualized instruction.

One of the most compelling prospects is creating an AI-enabled global digital library, a comprehensive repository of all human knowledge. This resource would democratize access to information, breaking down barriers related to geography, socioeconomic status, or institutional constraints.

However, it is crucial to acknowledge that our current education system has struggled to keep pace with rapid technological advancements. A significant disconnect exists between the knowledge imparted in schools and the skills required to thrive in the real world. This gap has left students ill-prepared for the demands and challenges of today's dynamic professional landscape.

AI is poised to revolutionize education, transforming it from a static, one-size-fits-all model to a dynamic, individualized, and globally accessible platform. The advent of AI in education heralds an era of unprecedented possibilities and opportunities for learners worldwide.

Intuitive experience

Artificial intelligence often provides an intuitive user experience thanks to the remarkable advances in machine learning and cognitive computing technologies. These innovations are now accessible to anyone with a laptop, making it an exciting time to explore the vast potential of AI. However, fears persist about its potential to replace jobs or suppress individuality. Conversely, others see artificial intelligence as just another tool in the technological arsenal of humanity, meant to be used responsibly.

The world is evolving rapidly, and many are captivated by the transformative potential of AI. The fusion of human intuition and AI technology could usher in a new era of service and support in education. Artificial technology is changing how we interact and how we feel about these interactions. As robots become more humanlike, they make us more comfortable and even happier to accept their assistance.

Specifically, AI can provide higher-level support in education that humans alone cannot achieve. By analyzing real-time data, AI can anticipate problems before they occur and determine the next course of action more quickly. It can solve problems faster than ever, facilitating enhanced learning experiences for students worldwide.

The combination of human intuition and artificial intelligence offers an unparalleled experience. Humans provide an emotional connection, making people feel cared for and valued, while AI brings analytical prowess, identifying trends and patterns. Education is one sector experiencing this seismic shift, with AI poised to disrupt traditional teaching methods.

Imagine a classroom where AI replaces textbooks with interactive virtual environments. Students could solve math problems or read stories by engaging in complex processes. This evolution in education frees up time for other activities, fostering a more holistic learning experience.

The scope of AI's impact on education is boundless. Its primary role will be to augment human capabilities, enabling us to accomplish more with less effort and time. As a proactive assistant, AI can take on tasks traditionally reserved for experts or those who have dedicated extensive time to study, genuinely revolutionizing the education landscape.

How can human intuition be used with artificial intelligence technology?

Human intuition is a unique trait that AI technology cannot replicate. For instance, after years of using Facebook, users can intuitively sense when a friend's unusual post about their health struggles signals something serious based on previous interactions. This innate ability allows humans to make well-informed decisions, often surpassing the capabilities of machines.

Programmed to follow logical instructions, artificial intelligence lacks this level of creativity and flexibility. However, some researchers envision a future where human intelligence and AI work in harmony, with humans deciding based on insights gathered by AI. The potential of human intelligence extends beyond formal education, and computers would be significantly limited if solely reliant on human programming and interaction.

Rather than fearing AI as a job killer, we should consider how we can harmoniously blend our intuition with this technology. One possibility is a self-thinking computer system that operates independently without human input, like Siri on an iPhone. Alternatively, we could augment human capabilities through digital extensions like Google Glasses, which can help visually impaired individuals navigate electronic information and physical spaces.

Despite the exponential progress in computing, significant room for growth remains. AI is transforming education, with teaching bots managing classrooms and tracking student progress. Though a human touch remains essential in certain areas, they could automate the entire process, from instruction to grading.

Artificial intelligence can also manage traditionally labor-intensive tasks like scheduling conferences or generating real-time student progress reports. We can harmonize human instincts with supervised machine learning by viewing AI as an extension rather than replacing human intuition.

It is important to remember a few principles: recognize each party's strengths, use these complementary skill sets together, focus on improving communication, and be ready to adjust as needed.

It is commonly misunderstood that AI will rapidly take over humans as machines are more reliable. However, AI relies on our data to learn through trial and error. Combining AI-driven machine learning with human intuition allows companies to understand individual customer behavior while boosting productivity. AI's incorporation into sectors like translation or marketing makes its entry into education inevitable.

Companies and communities have already demonstrated AI's potential in language learning. High-tech education systems like Khan Academy and language learning apps like Duolingo utilize AI to enhance teaching.[56,57] For example, Coursera uses machine learning to assign tasks based on student competence levels.[58]

The implications for education are profound: AI could outperform humans in knowledge retention and understanding complex concepts. Consequently, schools are adopting AI technology early to assist students, promoting equality in education. While AI can aid us in many areas, it is essential to acknowledge that humans still excel in certain aspects.

When things go awry, the question arises—who is to blame? The human or the algorithm? This dilemma underscores the need to refine human intuition before it is entirely replaced. While autonomous car accidents make headlines, thousands of human-caused accidents occur daily, indicating our heightened sensitivity to machine errors. Overcoming this mistrust of AI is a hurdle, but with time, we may realize that living with artificial intelligence is preferable to living without it.

---

[56]. Khan Academy, 2021, (https://www.khanacademy.org/).
[57]. Duolingo, 2021, Learn a language for free (https://www.duolingo.com/).
[58]. Coursera, 2021, "Online Courses & Credentials from Top Educators" 2021 (https://www.coursera.org/).

CHAPTER 4

Educators and Teachers

Aims of educators and teachers

Reflecting on the world in which our children live, we are compelled to ask: How can we best prepare them for the future? While AI technology brings specific concerns, these can be mitigated by limiting its use and being aware of potential risks. Preparing for this technological shift is crucial and a task that should be undertaken immediately. Ensuring that all students have access to computers in school and understand how to use AI is an essential first step.

In addition, we need to educate ourselves and our communities about the applications of AI. As we consider the impact on our children, it becomes clear that we must proactively adapt to the impending technological changes that will permeate every aspect of our lives. It is incumbent upon us to ensure that our children have access to AI in education. If we fail to update our teaching methods now, we risk creating a vast divide between those who understand and can use AI and those who cannot.

The internet offers scores of resources for learning about AI, but access to these resources is not evenly distributed. It is our responsibility to identify those in need of assistance and provide them with the resources required to understand and protect themselves in the digital age. While AI can be deployed across various industries, the ultimate goal should always be to improve outcomes. AI encompasses an array of facets, such as machine learning and deep learning. However, we must also question its accuracy and consider the limitations of AI, including biases, decision-making complexities, and ethical concerns surrounding automation, before integrating it into our lives.

The potential impact of AI on teachers' job prospects is a subject of ongoing debate among educators. Some believe AI could replace their roles, while others view it as a tool to enhance teaching methods through immediate feedback on student performance. The eventual impact of AI remains uncertain, but one thing is clear: there are no straightforward answers at present.

So, how can teachers foster better classroom conversations? Establishing routines, facilitating dialogue, and encouraging active student participation is a crucial first step. Teachers can guide discussions, using natural pauses to introduce new ideas or alternative perspectives. Creating a judgment-free environment where teachers and students feel comfortable expressing their thoughts is also vital.

Engaging with students' families can significantly enhance their learning experience. Teachers should build collaborative relationships with parents, focusing on academic progress and promoting student well-being. This task might prove challenging, particularly for students who are shy around their peers, but it is an integral part of a teacher's role.

Future educators: robots

Education, a cornerstone of our society, spans from kindergarten to the boardroom. Integrating artificial intelligence into classrooms is a promising avenue as we ponder ways to enhance this crucial pillar. This technology could revolutionize the way teachers and students interact and learn.

Education has been the bedrock of knowledge and growth since the dawn of civilization. But what if our future educators weren't humans but AI-powered robots? The impact of AI on various sectors of our society has been profound, leading some to wonder if it should extend its reach into education.

While the concept of AI educators may seem enticing to many, it is essential to consider the implications. For instance, would a child prefer to be taught by a disengaged teacher, weary from the demands of their profession, or by an AI, devoid of human warmth but consistently efficient? While we may not be entirely ready for this transition, the reality of AI playing a significant role in education is fast approaching.

Given the ubiquity of AI in our daily lives, from smartphones to home assistants, it is hardly surprising that there's interest in its educational applications. Imagine a world where education transcends the boundaries of traditional classrooms and textbooks. Imagine a time when AI served as our teachers and mentors, shaping us into informed adults. What implications would this have for society?

In this potential era of AI educators, new opportunities could emerge. Students could gain access to diverse experiences and perspectives from around the globe. Lessons could become more personalized and tailored to each student's unique learning needs and preferences—a trend already evident in some schools.

This shift could also ease pressure on parents and caregivers, freeing children to engage in extracurricular activities like sports or the arts. However, such a radical transformation in learning methods may also have unintended consequences. For instance, AI educators would need to be programmed with cultural sensitivity, given the global nature of online education.

Students could enroll in multiple online courses simultaneously, irrespective of geographical constraints. In a dystopian scenario, AI could be programmed to monitor and control all aspects of education, potentially limiting academic freedom. As we navigate this brave new world of AI-driven education, balancing technological advances with ethical considerations and preserving the human touch in learning is crucial.

AI taking over the role of educators

Imagine a future where artificial intelligence assumes the role of an educator. This intriguing concept prompts us to ponder: What would happen to our education system if AI replaced human teachers? What types of experiences would students who are used to interacting with human educators have?

Many parents might wonder how an AI teacher would interact with their children. AI can provide personalized feedback based on each student's work with its adaptive algorithms. One significant advantage of employing AI as an educator could be dramatically reduced education costs. However, this shift would undeniably have enormous repercussions, prompting questions about the potential impacts.

Consider its application in language learning to better understand the transformative changes AI could introduce into current school practices. Artificial intelligence could provide opportunities for children to excel beyond traditional academic standards by challenging them at higher levels. This could lead to improved test scores and expedite educational completion.

Undoubtedly, AI technology will significantly impact how we acquire knowledge. It promises to accelerate learning and invigorate subjects that might seem dull or overwhelming due to their complexity. Imagine having a wealth of knowledge at our fingertips—solving math problems like Einstein or learning Spanish through interactive Rosetta Stone videos.[59] The possibilities are endless.

Artificial intelligence could revolutionize education by teaching foreign languages via conversational bots or interactive video games. This could improve global connections, vital in today's world, where many live far from their homelands. It could also help students become fluent in languages critical for international business.

---

[59]. Official Rosetta Stone® 2021, Language Learning - Learn a Language (https://www.rosettastone.com/).

This new technological era heralds unprecedented learning opportunities and monumental shifts across all work sectors. It can enhance student learning by providing personalized educational materials based on their abilities and needs, determined by assessments at the start of each academic year or semester. This approach improves retention rates by tailoring lessons to individual needs, reducing homework loads, and minimizing boredom.

Integrating AI into education has already begun transforming lives and will continue to evolve. Google's TensorFlow project, which teaches students about AI, has sparked positive changes in education and creativity.[60] With a greater emphasis on STEM programs and arts integration in classrooms across America, the potential achievements with these powerful tools are limitless.

Regarding employment, it may be necessary to retrain workers displaced by AI for emerging job types. This could require a significant overhaul of education delivery, encompassing lifelong learning or short-term retraining programs. A technology that understands human cognitive processes has arrived in classrooms—artificial intelligence. Schools can now utilize deep neural networks and advanced programming drawn from neuroscience research to facilitate more efficient learning than traditional methods.

While contemplating AI as a teacher substitute, we must consider potential drawbacks. For instance, AI could become an elitist tool accessible only to those who can afford it, exacerbating socioeconomic disparities. As robotic teachers are expensive, they may not be accessible to all.

Artificial intelligence has the potential to revolutionize education by connecting teachers and students worldwide.[61] It can assist teach-

---

60. TensorFlow 2021, (https://www.tensorflow.org/).
61. Marr, B., "How Is AI Used in Education—Real World Examples of Today and a Peek into the Future" *Forbes*, 2018, (https://www.forbes.com/sites/bernard-marr/2018/07/25/how-is-ai-used-in-education-real-world-examples-of-today-and-a-peek-into-the-future/?sh=184e8b0b586e).

ers in grading papers and tests, delivering lectures, and even answering questions. Artificial intelligence can aid students who struggle with voice use or reading text on a screen. By utilizing artificial neural networks to simulate human thought patterns, AI can offer a more intuitive user experience. This revolution in education will transform how we learn and enrich everyday life.

If specific predictions are made, we may soon witness a future where AI is integral to every facet of education. While this prospect excites some, others harbor apprehensions. Many experts predict significant changes in the service industry by 2025 due to advances in AI and robotics.[62] This could eliminate the need for human labor, as computers might outperform us in every task.

Artificial intelligence is rapidly transforming various aspects of our lives—from how we work to how we interact with technology. Its potential influence on education is equally significant, poised to usher in a new era where advanced AI systems do not just answer questions and solve problems but also make critical decisions. These systems could revolutionize all aspects of life, including education, by operating as personal management assistants. It is becoming increasingly clear that integrating AI into education can enhance human intelligence, and we have already begun to see positive results.

The transformation of education through AI can be envisioned in three critical steps. The first involves developing systems where machines learn from interactions between teachers, students, educational content, and other factors such as location or time. The second step entails integrating these personalized services into existing platforms, making them readily accessible for educational purposes. Finally, it will fundamentally alter how people learn, think, and process information, leading to a profound shift in our educational paradigms.

---

[62]. Smith A. and Anderson, J. "Predictions for the State of AI and Robotics in 2025" Pew Research Center, 2014, (https://www.pewresearch.org/internet/2014/08/06/predictions-for-the-state-of-ai-and-robotics-in-2025/).

The implications of AI in education are indeed vast. The impact of these advancements will reverberate through generations, offering staggering potential. However, a more formalized approach is necessary to maximize the positive effects while mitigating potential downsides. This strategy should consider the interests of various stakeholders and assess ethical considerations at every developmental stage. Integrating technology at all educational levels could pivot us from rote memorization to critical thinking and problem-solving. With AI in classrooms, educators can make informed decisions about when and how to integrate this transformative technology.

However, implementing AI in education is not without its challenges. Concerns have been raised about potential biases.[63] For instance, if AI is deployed in classrooms, ensuring nondiscrimination against certain students is crucial. Human teachers will continue to play a vital role in providing emotional support and guidance. Additionally, claims that human teachers may become obsolete within twenty to thirty years as computers take over their duties raise concerns about potential biases in teaching methods, which could negatively impact our society. We must remain vigilant and take proactive steps to prevent these potential biases.

Another challenge lies in the lack of standardization in AI educational programs, which complicates comparisons between different programs and makes it difficult for employers to find out the skills a student has acquired. We must strive toward creating standards for AI education programs to ensure everyone can reap the benefits.

We must also contemplate the ethical implications of using AI in education. For example, should AI be employed to grade students? What would be the potential impact on student learning? And what are the implications of using AI to create personalized learning experiences? These pertinent questions warrant thorough consideration before implementing AI in education.

---

[63]. Tuomi, Ilkka, "The Impact of Artificial Intelligence on Learning, Teaching, and Education" 2018, (https:/doi:10.2760/12297).

Despite these challenges, the potential benefits of AI in education are too compelling to overlook. By teaching students in innovative ways, such as through virtual reality or adaptive learning, AI can ensure they receive the best possible education. If we can successfully navigate these challenges, AI has the potential to transform education for the better.

Teachers' concerns

Educators increasingly grapple with integrating artificial intelligence into their curricula. Amid growing apprehension that robots and AI may supplant classroom teachers, one potential solution is fostering human-robot collaboration within educational environments. This approach allows humans to focus on their strengths while machines oversee specific tasks such as grading tests or correcting spelling errors.

Such a strategy could enhance the emotional connection between students and teachers. With specific responsibilities delegated to technology, teachers could devote more time to inspiring young minds about their subjects. Consequently, students can learn mathematics, science, or languages from their new educational robot. Teachers, setting the AI objectives, can tailor their curriculum to cater to diverse student needs.

For instance, teachers could remotely monitor their classes via a video feed from another room at school or even from home. If any issues arise, they can promptly address them without physically needing to be there—a significant shift from traditional teaching methods.

However, a study revealed that teachers harbor concerns about AI's potential to diminish human interaction in education. Some fear that computers could replace them, offering a cost-effective alternative to underfunded classrooms.[64] As AI enters the education scene,

---

64. Brynjolfsson, Erik and Andrew McAfee, The Second Machine Age: Work, Progress, and Prosperity in a Time of Brilliant Technologies (New York City: W. W. Norton & Company, 2014).

opinions are divided—some view it as an engaging and valuable experience, while others see it as potentially limiting.[65]

Therefore, teachers must understand how AI will impact their profession and what steps they can take to prepare. With technologies like automated teaching systems emerging, educators need to stay current with skills such as programming. They can then instruct students in various ways without solely relying on standardized tests or curriculum knowledge.

These new teaching tools present both challenges and opportunities. Freed from traditional pedagogy constraints, educators could innovatively leverage AI-based software, enhancing their creativity. The careful integration of technology into classrooms will require thoughtful consideration from teachers. However, investment from critical stakeholders such as governments, parents, and school administrators could make cognitive computing technologies integral to revolutionizing education through AI.

Unquestionably, introducing AI into schools has its pros and cons. On the positive side, the management of administrative tasks can save teachers valuable time. However, it might also reduce student-teacher interaction as more students turn to technology for faster learning. How this shift affects academic performance is yet to be seen.

Artificial intelligence has been used to create simulations and virtual worlds, influencing how students learn, their attitudes toward school, and their emotional well-being outside the classroom. Concerned that these new programs or algorithms might replace them, teachers are exploring ways to integrate technology without losing the essence of their teaching methods. One approach already in practice is introducing robots as part of an interactive classroom environment. Here, children engage with them on multiple levels—from socializing and building projects to acquiring mechanical skills to prepare for real-life jobs in STEM fields.

---

65. Willis, P., "Should Computers Replace Teachers in Class?" 2019, (https://study.com/blog/should-computers-replace-teachers-in-class.html).

Using AI to detect depression in teachers

1. Detecting depression in teachers through voice tone.

Artificial intelligence could be revolutionary in diagnosing notoriously elusive mental illnesses like depression. Voice analysis software, for instance, can detect signs of mental conditions such as depression and anxiety, even without knowing the user's background or circumstances.[66] This AI technology identifies changes in tone and intonation as users speak on their phones or computers. Analyzing data points on speech patterns uncovers evidence too subtle for human interpretation. Subsequently, AI can assist individuals undergoing cognitive behavioral therapy—an approach that equips them with skills to manage their condition more effectively and reduce the risk of relapse.

The application of AI in diagnosing depression is not merely conceptual; it already exists in practice. For example, an application has been developed that detects depression among teachers by analyzing their tone of voice.[67] This is crucial, as many educators worldwide silently grapple with depression, often unaware of their condition due to deeply buried symptoms. This poses a significant problem, as teachers' mental health affects their well-being and their students' academic performance. The teaching profession has historically exhibited higher-than-average rates of mental illness.

The prevalence of mental health issues among teachers is hardly surprising. A recent study from the UCL Institute of Education reported that one in every twenty teachers (or 5 percent) is likely to experience a long-term illness, adversely impacting their work and

---

66. Tazrout, Z., "Voice analysis on a smartphone to detect signs of a depressive disorder Actu IA" 2021, (https://www.bing.com/search?q=Voice+analysis+on+a+smartphone+to+detect+signs+of+a+depressive+disorder+-+Actu+IA&cvid=30dab38c452a45639ecd0c9a19c4f26f&aqs=edge..69i57j69i60.628j0j4&FORM=ANAB01&PC=LCTS).

67. Fagherazzi, G., Fischer, A., Ismael,M. and Despotovic, V., *Voice for Health: The Use of Vocal Biomarkers from Research to Clinical Practice* Digital Biomarkers 2021, Vol. 5, No. 1, (Karger Publishers, https:// doi: 10.1159/000515346).

students' learning experiences.[68] The pressures of teaching, including full-time responsibilities and relatively lower wages compared to other professions requiring similar education or skill levels, are contributing factors. Some educators require care even during working hours, while others have opted for early retirement before seeking help due to cognitive symptoms caused by stress and fatigue.

A depressed teacher may exhibit reduced creativity in class, resulting in lower student grades. Moreover, teachers dealing with depression often display monotone and sluggish speech patterns. While these low-energy speech characteristics have been studied for decades to gain insight into mental health disorders like schizophrenia or bipolar disorder, they are now used as an early detection method to identify conditions before they escalate to severe problems like absenteeism or suicide attempts.

However, the advent of AI offers a beacon of hope. It extends beyond the workplace, potentially serving as a crucial component in mental health treatment efforts within the education sector. Professor John Jerrim from the UCL Institute of Education commented, "The results from our study may not be as worrying if it means more teachers struggling with mental health get help. But the profession needs further monitoring and improvement of well-being—like what has been done for tracking workloads over time."[69]

Cognitive behavioral therapy (CBT) can effectively manage mental illnesses like depression and anxiety.[70] Previously, many individuals felt isolated, frequently unaware of the potential impacts on themselves and others. This could lead to depression, anxiety attacks, or

---

[68]. Nuffield Foundation "More teachers are reporting mental health problems than ever" 2020, (https://www.nuffieldfoundation.org/news/more-teachers-reporting-mental-health-problems-than-ever).

[69]. University College London, "More teachers reporting mental health problems" 2020, (https://www.ucl.ac.uk/news/2020/jan/more-teachers-reporting-mental-health-problems).

[70]. Cherry, K., Cognitive Behavioral Therapy (CBT): Definition, Types, Techniques, Efficiency, 2021, (https://www.verywellmind.com/what-is-cognitive-behavior-therapy-2795747).

even worse, with no warning signs before significantly disrupting their work life.

Artificial intelligence is confronting this issue directly by providing immediate support through AI chatbots that offer comforting words and daily reminders to those dealing with mental health issues. It allows access to resources via mobile apps and online giving platforms, which fund mental health advocacy organizations worldwide. These platforms educate individuals on better understanding and addressing future mental health issues.

2. Detecting depression in teachers through facial expression.

Face detection technology, powered by advanced AI algorithms, could soon serve as an early warning system for depression among school faculty members. By tracking facial neural activity, this innovative technology can detect subtle signs of mood swings, such as sadness or stress, even when someone attempts to mask these feelings.

This breakthrough was achieved by applying machine learning techniques to thousands of videos captured from various angles and distances. Teachers, who often face mental challenges due to their deep concern for their students, are the primary targets of this technology. Such emotional investment may result in compassion fatigue syndrome (CFS), a condition marked by guilt or sympathy for those who are suffering.

Recent studies have linked teachers' anxiety, depression, and suicide levels to their work environment, prompting schools to investigate methods for identifying struggling educators. For instance, facial recognition software can pick up emotional cues such as asymmetrical lip movements or exposed teeth.

Schools are exploring novel approaches, such as deploying camera technology to recognize emotions based on facial expressions. This includes identifying signs of depression, like one side of the mouth drooping. This investigative research has gained urgency due to the alarming increase in suicides among educators who reported feeling overwhelmed.

The researchers developed a facial recognition system to identify signs of depression among teachers on school premises. The goal is to allow schools and administrators to offer support before the situation escalates into more severe symptoms like attempted suicide or alcoholism. These conditions would necessitate costly interventions like counseling services. If further testing validates this research, it could significantly contribute to maintaining educators' physical and mental health, enabling them to perform their duties effectively without the debilitating interference of depression.

Machine learning provides scientists with a unique lens to interpret the subtle movements of facial expressions. For instance, researchers at Carnegie Mellon University employ a multimodal algorithm that analyzes sixty-eight points on the face, including eyebrows, eye corners, and the mouth. This precise analysis makes it possible to discern thoughts and emotions. The researchers are interested in using machine learning to trace connections between facial expressions and emotional states among depressed individuals.[71]

A study titled "Extraction of Facial Features for Depression Detection Among Students" offers another promising approach. This research proposes a system designed to detect depression in college students, which could be extrapolated to teachers. This system is trained using images of people expressing various emotions, such as happiness, anger, or disgust. During the testing phase, videos of college students answering questionnaires are collected. Facial features are extracted from these videos and normalized. The features are then classified by a support vector machine (SVM), a well-known classifier for depression detection. Based on the presence of negative expressions and the scarcity of happy features, the student is assigned a degree of depression ranging from mild to high.

---

[71]. LaFrance, A. "Machines That Can See Depression on a Person's Face" 2015, (https://www.theatlantic.com/technology/archive/2015/10/machines-that-can-see-depression-on-a-persons-face/411229/).

The level of depression will be determined by how much negativity is in the video. Lower levels of happy features result in increased levels of negativity. In addition, students exhibiting high negativity levels will be classified as highly depressed, moderate negativity levels will be classified as mildly depressed, and low negativity levels are not depressed.[72]

This system holds immense potential for identifying more severe symptoms, such as suicidal tendencies or self-harming behavior. Monitoring physical symptoms of depression could indeed save lives, underscoring the importance of investing in such life-changing technologies.

---

[72]. Venkataraman, D., Parameswaran, N. "Extraction of Facial Features for Depression Detection among Students" *International Journal of Pure and Applied Mathematics* 2018, Volume 118 No. 7 2018, p. 455–463, Retrieved from (https://acadpubl.eu/jsi/2018-118-7-9/articles/7/61.pdf?msclkid=17b11eb8a83211ec85105e2f409d223f).

CHAPTER 5

Students

What we can do to help students

The advent of artificial intelligence in education necessitates a seismic change in teaching methodologies to prevent students from being underserved. This imminent change might seem like a distant concern, but it is already happening.

Data analysis has emerged as a top marketable skill for students. However, acquiring this proficiency within the confines of a conventional four-year degree program is becoming increasingly challenging. Resistance to change is a common human trait, and many students balk at consuming course materials digitally. This reluctance often stems from a lack of trust in new technologies and ideas, exacerbated by past experiences of disappointment with unreliable systems or individuals.

Educators typically perceive this resistance as opposition, causing them to hesitate to deploy technology as an educational tool. But what if this perceived conflict could be viewed as an opportunity for dialogue and creative exploration of "new ways"? Instead of adhering strictly to traditional methods, educators could engage with their students to discover innovative solutions.

The ultimate aim is not to replace teachers with AI but to improve educational outcomes by leveraging AI for inquiry learning, natural language processing, and computer vision. Machine learning allows a system to acquire data without explicit programming and to improve with experience over time.[73] Natural language processing defines how computers can process human languages, such as speech or written text, by analyzing grammatical structures and words to form sentences of their own that are indistinguishable from any human.

Computer vision is a machine's ability to use cameras or other sensors to see an object, person, text, etcetera, and generate a high-quality image from it with enough detail for AI systems to understand.[74]

Indeed, these technologies are already having significant impacts on educational institutions worldwide. Some argue that we are entering a new era where computers may soon surpass humans as educators. While the future led by AI might be better in terms of efficiency, cost-effectiveness, and inclusivity, there are some drawbacks to keep in mind.

One concern is that if computers become the primary source of knowledge, children might grow up reliant solely on these machines for learning. Another issue is that those who are already privileged might benefit from AI in education more than others, perpetuating educational inequalities. Furthermore, the question arises about how we use the knowledge that machines gather for us.

Viewing AI as a supplement for teachers, not a replacement, is essential. Measuring success in an AI-driven educational environment is a challenge. It is not enough to know that a child is learning; their progress needs to be quantifiable, and the feedback should be relayed to the learner.

---

[73]. "Machine learning and financial institutions" VISA CONSULTING & ANALYTICS, 2019, (https://all-lb.visa.com/partner-with-us/visa-consulting-analytics/machine-learning-and-financial-institutions.html).

[74]. IBM "What is Computer Vision?" (https://www.ibm.com/topics/computer-vision?msclkid=7fa75259a82811ec87bc171eeb2bde4a).

While introducing AI into classrooms, we must consider potential drawbacks such as a lack of human interaction, teacher job displacement, reduced creativity, and ethical issues like unequal exam time allocations based on racial or economic backgrounds.[75] As a forward-thinking society, we should encourage educators and students to consider how these new technologies can positively and creatively disrupt education.

The arrival of advanced computers in classrooms over the next decade will complicate education and potentially disadvantage marginalized groups. We must also consider the limitations of AI, such as its inability to produce original ideas. Are students destined to learn everything through a series of algorithms, limited by what computers teach? These are the critical questions that educators must grapple with as we navigate the exciting yet challenging landscape of AI in education.

Artificial intelligence is an exceptional learner, but its learning capacity hinges on its instruction, which limits creativity. It operates through algorithms and preprogrammed instructions, lacking emotional intelligence or independent thinking, which are crucial in tailoring education to individual students' needs.

The potential of AI in education is both exhilarating and daunting, given its wide-ranging applications and ethical considerations. For instance, machine learning can expedite essay grading, a task traditionally performed by humans. Furthermore, AI can predict a student's academic performance, providing valuable insights for tailored learning experiences. However, if misused, these predictions could potentially lead to discrimination.

These exciting advantages and ethical concerns necessitate thoughtful deliberation before AI's implementation in education. Equally important is the accuracy and bias-free nature of the data

---

[75]. Pedró, F., Subosa, M., Rivas, A., "Artificial intelligence in education: challenges and opportunities for sustainable development" UNESCO Digital Library, 2019, (https://unesdoc.unesco.org/ark:/48223/pf0000366994).

used to train AI systems. Inaccurate or biased data could lead to unjust decisions about students, especially those from marginalized groups.

Another concern is the potential job displacement due to AI's increasing role in education. For instance, if AI can grade essays more efficiently than humans, this could reduce teaching positions. Therefore, the implications of AI on employment must be carefully considered before integrating it into classrooms.

Despite these challenges, the rapid evolution of AI promises to reshape the educational landscape. Artificial intelligence can be a powerful ally in identifying students with learning difficulties, allowing resources to be channeled effectively. For example, machine learning and deep neural networks have been deployed to predict academic success among students with learning difficulties and language impairments such as dyslexia. It also opens possibilities for innovative courses, teaching children about programming, internet functionality, and the world around them. It can enhance their understanding of diverse cultures, history, science, mathematics, and other subjects. Moreover, AI can improve children's reading and writing skills, stimulate critical thinking, foster creativity, and teach them about music and art.

The arrival of AI in education has amplified interest in STEM fields (science, technology, engineering, and math) and spurred a growing trend of teaching MOOCs (massive open online courses) using AI.[76] This approach offers multiple benefits, including access to expert lectures in transcript format and previously unavailable data about teaching.

However, there are challenges to overcome. Data quality and relevance can vary significantly; providing students with only the nec-

---

[76]. MOOC.org. Massive Open Online Courses An edX Site (https://www.mooc.org/).

essary information is essential. This calls for accurate content recognition to facilitate personalized instruction.[77] Emerging technologies like augmented reality and machine learning algorithms will shape future classrooms, promoting customized education and fostering human innovation.

Do students miss the interaction with the human teacher?

Education is a powerful tool for self-improvement and the betterment of one's family. With the dawn of artificial intelligence in education, we must find ways to ensure this transformation does not disadvantage students but instead benefits them. For instance, maintaining social connections between students and instructors can prove challenging, particularly in an online learning environment. The absence of interpersonal interactions can harm both parties involved in the teaching process.

Without communicating directly or seeing each other's facial expressions, instructors may struggle to guide their students during distance learning, and vice versa. This means some individuals may not take an online course seriously due to potential technical glitches and the necessity for full attention throughout the learning process. A significant concern is the possible loss of personal interactions, where students receive direct feedback on their work and engage in meaningful dialogue with their instructors. So, how can we utilize AI to personalize the learning experience and improve people's lives?

The education sector faces numerous challenges in this digital age. Although AI cannot wholly replace teachers, it can enhance the educational experience through human interaction. The traditional classroom setting becomes less prevalent as more students engage with social media, streaming videos, and remote lectures through

---

77. Marr, B., "How Is AI Used in Education—Real World Examples of Today and a Peek Into the Future" *Forbes*, 2018, (https://www.forbes.com/sites/bernard-marr/2018/07/25/how-is-ai-used-in-education-real-world-examples-of-today-and-a-peek-into-the-future/?sh=184e8b0b586e).

online courses. However, with AI continually evolving and providing interactive dialogues for educators and their students, there is hope for improved learning experiences.

One proposed solution is using AI to provide feedback on critical assignments outside of school hours. However, it is vital to ensure the accuracy of the content delivered in an online course when using AI as a learning resource. This could be achieved by having a committee of teachers review the material before making it available on the platform or by employing a teacher's assistant to support and monitor student progress throughout the course.

Teachers play a crucial role in this new educational landscape and require additional training to maintain human interactions with students during their formative years. Artificial intelligence can support teachers by making lessons interactive, engaging, and personalized for students. It does this by tracking student progress and providing individualized feedback, ensuring they are on the right path.

However, not everyone agrees that AI should replace teachers or dominate classrooms. Instead, we need to explore ways for students to experience a mix of face-to-face and virtual interactions while receiving AI support. It is time for educators to consider alternative models, such as blended learning, which combines online and in-class courses.

Human-centered design principles are essential in this context because, while algorithms can guide teachers and students through activities, they should not replace the human element of education. These AI algorithms should be viewed as tools designed to support educators when needed most, enhancing the teaching and learning experience.

Will students miss the interaction with a human teacher?

Artificial intelligence can create personalized tutorials and custom-tailored courses based on individual students' needs. This eliminates unnecessary repetition for those who have mastered the material and provides a faster catch-up mechanism for those who require it. However, as technology advances and the demand for human teachers decreases, questions arise about whether students will miss interactions with a human teacher.

This predicament elicits varied responses. Some students favor human teachers over technology, citing that they offer more freedom, closer interaction, and a personal touch, often surpassing what AI can offer. Meanwhile, other students gravitate toward online learning due to its convenience and flexibility, requiring no commute to school. Such students are typically disciplined, independent, and study oriented.

Yet a group prefers traditional classrooms because they offer more opportunities for social interaction than their virtual counterparts. To address these varying preferences, many colleges have adopted blended learning, which combines both traditional classroom settings and online classes.

This approach aligns with current research, suggesting that student interaction can be beneficial or detrimental, depending on the student's goals. Interestingly, these interactions frequently prove less crucial than studying outside the classroom. One question that comes up is whether or not students would make friends in a class with a virtual teacher. While this may seem absurd to those accustomed to traditional schooling, the answer is unclear for the current generation of students.

The future of AI-driven classrooms filled with conversation and laughter is still uncertain. The prevalent opinion favors human teachers, as they provide individual attention and help students develop social skills that cannot be learned from a virtual teacher. However, there are instances where virtual-led classes surpass traditional ones in effectiveness.

The prospect of installing robots in every classroom is dramatic and raises questions about how it might impact student interaction.

Many argue for teacher support systems to prevent things from spiraling out of control.

The rationale behind this sweeping change in the education system lies in the data. Robots can instruct students, gather valuable information about their learning, track their progress, and adapt to their needs, resulting in more successful students.

While concerns about missing human interaction are valid, AI teaching could benefit some students with specific needs and disabilities. For instance, robots can ensure no background noise, aiding people with auditory processing issues or other hearing impairments.

Despite our digital age, we believe that human interactions remain essential. With over two-thirds of classrooms using screen time for learning purposes, there is a concern about students missing out on vital interaction with human teachers. Learning labs can supplement this interaction, allowing students to tackle complex problems, discuss problem-solving methods, and delve into course content. Such interactions enable students to identify gaps in their knowledge and address them. They also benefit from interacting with peers grappling with similar challenges or excelling in the same classes, offering fresh perspectives. While some students are excited about AI teachers due to their accessibility, most worry about losing social interaction, a cherished part of school life.

It is worth reminiscing about the good old days of school when teachers talked to students and gave them individualized attention. There is a correlation between classroom engagement and subsequent achievement or interest. Teachers who spend more time discussing topics rather than providing short answers facilitate better absorption of the material, especially for children whose language skills may not yet be fully developed. In such cases, direct communication provides support, preventing frustration and promoting continued learning.

What does it mean if we lose these interactions? The human teacher fosters a child's growth and social development through one-on-one interactions, regardless of the setting. These interactions often enable them to learn faster than they would by watching a video or reading a book. If these interactions with teachers are lost, students may spend more time in front of screens and less time learning from our most valuable resource—other humans. This could make children feel less socially connected or struggle to cope without direct guidance.

How will students learn social skills and emotional intelligence without direct contact with their teachers (or anyone else)? If students lack opportunities to interact with their teachers, there could be detrimental effects on their learning, conversational skills, and emotional intelligence. One potential solution is to leverage technology to facilitate remote communication between students and teachers. This would allow students to interact with their teacher while benefiting from virtual lessons. However, this approach is not without drawbacks.

A primary concern is that students may develop inadequate social skills due to the absence of physical interaction with peers and adults. This could pose challenges in their future endeavors, such as finding and retaining employment. Additionally, a lack of human interaction could diminish a student's emotional intelligence and conversational skills, increase the risk of cyberbullying, and exacerbate mental health issues due to the deprivation of therapeutic social interactions.

The advent of this new teaching methodology presents both advantages and disadvantages. Still, the most significant impact could be its potential disruption of traditional education by altering how people learn conversational skills and emotional intelligence. So, what is the solution? The answer depends on who you ask, but educational technology offers some promising ideas.

Some education experts suggest that the future might hold non-traditional classrooms where educational content is delivered via computer, with teachers available for assistance or guidance. However, others argue that replacing a human teacher's individualized touch and responsiveness is impossible. Both perspectives have their merits and drawbacks, leading to a crucial question: should we retain human interaction or transition to AI-driven education?

Privacy concerns are another issue. There are many worries about data ownership when using AI. Critics argue that the company owning the data could monopolize information and wield undue power over its users, potentially leading to discrimination or fraud.[78] While there is no definitive solution to these concerns due to the novelty of the issue, efforts can be made to guarantee equal access and privacy. Data has been aptly described as the new oil fueling the engine of societal progress.

One way to ensure everyone has easy accessibility is to make your datasets publicly available without restrictions. On the other hand, open availability can be established for facilities to make sure that the data is accessible to anyone at any time, as long as there is no infringement. If these options are unfeasible, technology could be developed to allow users to dictate their terms when dealing with digital content, such as negotiating price or usage.

Another potential pitfall of AI is bias. If data is not collected evenly from all groups of people, the resulting AI could lack representation, leading to empathy issues and hindering our understanding of diverse communities. For instance, privileged classes often harbor biases against the impoverished, which can infiltrate the data if not carefully managed. Consequently, these biases can perpetuate through AI models designed using this data.

In conclusion, it is important to remember that humans need connections. They need to feel like they have a friend or someone who cares about them. If society eliminates all social interaction, we may end up with individuals who feel disconnected. The one constant thing that has never changed is the need for human communication and connection; losing this would be devastating. Hence, while AI can significantly enhance the learning process, ensuring that it does not

---

78. Ahmed, H., 2021, "Challenges of AI and Data Privacy—And How to Solve Them" (https://www.isaca.org/resources/news-and-trends/newsletters/atisaca/2021/volume-32/challenges-of-ai-and-data-privacy-and-how-to-solve-them).

replace the enriching experience of human interaction in education is essential.

Using AI to detect depression in students

1. Detecting depression through voice tone.

Imagine a future where teachers can receive real-time feedback by analyzing their students' tone of voice. This innovative feature could enable them to identify better students struggling with depression and provide timely, targeted help that significantly impacts academic performance. Imagine an end to the era of teachers dismissing students' concerns despite glaring signs of distress. It could aid in procuring external support before a crisis as severe as suicide occurs. Furthermore, it could help identify the most effective therapeutic approach for those typically unable to vocalize their struggles or admit their need for assistance in a society that often encourages us to mask our difficulties.

Mental health care is a labyrinth of complexities, with numerous factors contributing to confusion, making diagnosis and treatment arduous. As technology advances, it paves the way for researchers to uncover innovative methods to comprehend and treat mental illnesses. Mental health is a sensitive issue that is typically challenging to discuss for those battling depression. However, with AI's potential to assist and support individuals suffering from this disease, several strategies for symptom detection have emerged.

One such method involves using the voice recognition capabilities of a mobile application, allowing mental health experts to provide round-the-clock assistance during challenging times or just before a mood slump. For instance, AI can detect depression through voice analysis, equipping teachers and other mental health professionals to make more informed decisions regarding their students' well-being.

Artificial intelligence technology can analyze volume, pitch, and cadence changes between syllables spoken by individuals with anxiety or depression.[79] These AI-based detection systems could revolutionize how educators support students with these conditions and simplify the task for parents caring for children grappling with these issues at home. While AI shows promise for assisting students, it is not a flawless solution. Nonetheless, it can be beneficial for adults, helping them maintain productivity and emotional stability at work or school until they can get proper treatment from a healthcare professional.

The Ellipsis program utilizes vocal features like pitch, cadence, and enunciation to scrutinize conversations for signs of depression.[80] Data scientists supplement this analysis with information from mental health questionnaires or clinical records to train their software on millions of voices. This enables it to recognize vocal features indicative of various emotional states, including happiness.

Moreover, AI can now mine text messages, emails, and social media platforms like Facebook Messenger and WhatsApp for signs of depression.[81] The system employs linguistic analysis through tone detection software that scrutinizes emotional phrases or key phrases often associated with mental illness, such as "I'm sorry" or "Nothing good happens," or frequency of usage.[82,83] With the recent advancements in artificial intelligence, it is not surprising that machines can be trained on speech recognition, providing a valuable tool for diagnosis and treatment planning.

---

79. Abinisha S., "AI Detect individual's mood by analyzing speech" 2017, (https://abinisha444com.wordpress.com/2017/02/05/ai-detect-individuals-mood-by-analysing-speech-5/?msclkid=448fec35a83511ec92cbc53f93333b48).

80. Smith, D., "Capturing the Sound of Depression in the Human Voice" 2017, (https://www.kqed.org/futureofyou/435986/capturing-the-sound-of-depression-in-the-human-voice).

81. Facebook, 2021, (https://www.facebook.com/).

82. Kesari, G., "AI Can Now Detect Depression from Your Voice, and It's Twice as Accurate as Human Practitioners" 2021, (https://www.forbes.com/sites/ganeskesari/2021/05/24/ai-can-now-detect-depression-from-just-your-voice/?sh=781e8c834c8d).

83. Stevens Institute of Technology, "Detecting Depression, Using AI" 2021, (https://www.stevens.edu/news/detecting-depression-using-ai).

To find patterns in spoken language and changes in pitch, volume, or pauses between words, researchers use computer systems and algorithms that are based on deep neural networks and biological nervous tissue. While humans typically overlook these signs, they can be remarkably indicative. These algorithms have successfully diagnosed clinical levels of depression among participants who had received a clinical diagnosis elsewhere. However, there are concerns that AI may over diagnose individuals with milder cases or diagnose those unaware of their condition. Moreover, this upheaval could plunge many students from low socioeconomic backgrounds, without access to therapy or counseling, into more profound despair.

For instance, researchers from St. Xavier's College, Kolkata, utilize AI trained through mood analysis and natural language processing.[84,85] They predict whether a patient may experience symptoms related to mental health disorders, such as anxiety or depressive episodes. The AI detects subtle changes in speech, such as tone and pace, while searching for deviations from what might be considered "normal."

However, it remains crucial for humans to recognize these signs. If you suspect someone may struggle with their mental health, take note of behavioral changes. For example, if an ordinarily outgoing individual suddenly becomes introverted or starts displaying rudeness, it could indicate a problem, signaling the time to intervene.

2. Detecting depression through facial expression.

Facial recognition technology is emerging as a powerful tool in schools, helping to identify students grappling with mental health issues such as depression, anxiety, and other conditions often triggered

---

84. Datta, D., Majumdar, S., Sen, O., International Journal of Innovative Technology and Exploring Engineering (IJITEE), Volume 9 Issue 2, December 2019, (https://doi: 10.35940/ijitee. B6158.129219).
85. Datta, D., Roy, A., Datta, S., Roy, U., International Journal of Soft Computing and Engineering, Volume 8 Issue 6, August 2019, (https:// doi: 10.35940/ijeat. F7987.088619).

by challenging learning experiences and educational hurdles. This innovative technology has already demonstrated its efficacy in detecting mood alterations in individuals with Alzheimer's. Consequently, it could potentially analyze subtle facial cues in students, indicating their struggle to cope with academic challenges.[86]

Facial expressions provide a window into an individual's emotional state. Therefore, this novel technology could significantly assist schools in monitoring student well-being. However, technology calls for enhancement in some areas. It does not adequately recognize all skin pigments, potentially leading to misidentification based on ethnicity unless personal information is provided beforehand.

Despite this shortcoming, technology holds immense potential as an early intervention tool, particularly in schools with high populations of struggling students. Preventing detrimental impacts on their mental health and academic outcomes can offer these students a lifeline. The software allows school administrations to screen potential cases by analyzing students' facial expressions. This enables timely intervention, offering much-needed support in educational settings and empowering teachers and staff members to take proactive measures.

One of the most effective strategies to mitigate depression levels in schools involves incorporating psychoeducational activities and interventions into the curriculum. These initiatives aim to foster self-awareness, challenge personal beliefs, enhance social relationships, and address other critical aspects of mental health. Numerous studies underscore the effectiveness of such programs, with participants scoring significantly lower on the Beck depression inventory than those who did not participate. This approach has proven successful in managing depression and should continue to be prioritized in our educational systems.

---

86. Torres, B., Simões, P., Sousa, M., Santos, R., "Facial Expression Recognition in Alzheimer's Disease: a Longitudinal Study" 2014, (https://doi:10.1590/0004-282X20150009).

Aaron Beck created the Beck's Depression Inventory (BDI, BDI-1A, BDI-II), a 21-question multiple-choice survey, in 1991. Its purpose is to gauge the severity of depressive symptoms in an individual.[87] This shift from viewing depression as solely a product of one's thoughts to acknowledging potential physical causes marks a significant advancement for mental health professionals. Before this, they primarily approached this condition with psychodynamic justifications.

Psychoeducational interventions empower students to independently explore their feelings and self-perceptions at their own pace and within their personal space. Mental health is a pressing issue demanding our attention. The arrival of this new technology will equip teachers with insights into each student's unique challenges, fostering a collaborative approach to addressing these mental health issues.

How we can help students who drop out of learning and are underachieving

Educators often assert that low achievement and school dropouts can be attributed to a lack of challenge from teachers and schoolwork. However, others argue that poor parenting plays a significant role in these issues.

There are myriad reasons why students underperform academically. Perhaps the student is not placed in a suitable class with a competent teacher or has disabilities, or familial circumstances may hinder them. Nevertheless, there are effective strategies to address these problems. For instance, educators can stimulate classroom participation and assign additional homework when necessary.

Motivation—or a lack—often lies at the root of underperformance. Even with a proficient mentor and superior teaching skills, success remains elusive without motivation. Generally, there are two types of motivation: intrinsic and extrinsic. Intrinsic motivation stems from within

---

87. American Psychological Association, "Beck Depression Inventory (BDI)" 2020, Updated 2021, (https://www.apa.org/pi/about/publications/caregivers/practice-settings/assessment/tools/beck-depression).

the individual—a curiosity about a subject or enjoyment derived from learning. On the contrary, external factors like parental pressure, rewards for achievement (such as grades), and punishments for failure (like detention) drive extrinsic motivation.

The most effective way to bolster motivation combines various methods and techniques. For example, educators can incorporate "playful learning" into lessons, weaving games, or puzzles into the curriculum to make it more interactive while disseminating information. Another approach involves posing "mastery" questions. These questions are challenging but answerable, instilling a sense of accomplishment in students when correctly answered, thereby enhancing their motivation.

However, how can we ensure children are not excluded from learning opportunities due to socioeconomic constraints? The solution lies in developing a systemic approach that guarantees all children, including those living in poverty, access to quality education. This could involve scholarships for higher education and resources for exceptionally talented students. Furthermore, creating an educational environment that embraces diverse teaching styles and backgrounds is crucial. Schools should also adopt open-field policies to encourage interaction between students and teachers, fostering collaboration, communication, and creativity, ultimately leading to improved learning outcomes.

Despite these measures, high school failure and dropout remain significant issues. In the United States alone, over 1.2 million students drop out of high school each year—approximately 7,000 per day or one student every 26 seconds.[88] This statistic does not account for those who dropped out before reaching twelfth grade or never attended in the first place. Hence, research into effective practices to prevent high school dropouts is vital.

In 2009, the number of "dropout factory" high schools—those graduating 60 percent or fewer students—was 1,634, according to a

---

[88]. "11 Facts About High School Dropout Rates" (https://www.dosome-thing.org/us/facts/11-facts-about-high-school-dropout-rates).

report released by America's Promise Alliance, Civic Enterprises, and Johns Hopkins University's Everyone Graduates Center. This figure represents a decrease from 1,746 in 2008 and a peak of 2,007 in 2002.[89] However, more efforts are needed to reduce this statistic further. These schools are problematic, with high crime rates among the students who drop out.

Effective practices to reverse chronic absenteeism include providing social and emotional support to students. Truancy solutions often prove ineffective, as absenteeism can stem from various causes, such as bullying. Therefore, programs designed to prevent school dropouts focus on regular attendance, keeping students engaged in their education, counseling, and vocational or social-emotional skills training.

Education is a primary focus worldwide, and America is no exception. Improving educational standards is paramount for social, economic, and cultural success. Implementing school guidance and tutoring practices can help achieve these goals, enabling schools to provide individualized instruction to struggling students or additional support from teachers when necessary.

The school dropout issue in Europe is complex, with numerous factors contributing to the challenge. The determinants and consequences of this phenomenon are multifaceted, as reasons for leaving school early can vary significantly from student to student. Factors such as learning difficulties, a lack of positive role models at home, and external influences like socioeconomic conditions can all play a pivotal role in a child's decision to discontinue their education post-high school graduation.[90]

In response to this growing concern, European countries have shifted their focus toward providing emotional and social support to these students. They have also been developing workplace initiatives

---

[89]. Paulson, A., "Fewer US schools qualify as 'dropout factories'" 2021, (https://www.csmonitor.com/USA/Education/2011/0322/Fewer-US-schools-qualify-as-dropout-factories).

[90]. Mashhad, M., "Combatting School Dropout in Europe United Way Worldwide" 2021, (https://www.unitedway.org/blog/combatting-school-dropout-in-europe#).

to engage disenfranchised youth and curb chronic absenteeism. However, schools are under resourced, lacking the teaching staff to effectively address the high dropout rates.

To mitigate these rates, schools must have sufficient resources to provide struggling students with the support they need. This could involve hiring additional teachers to offer personalized assistance, such as one-on-one tutoring. Practical school guidance and tutoring practices are crucial in addressing low achievement and high dropout rates.

Unfortunately, schools continue to grapple with the daunting challenge of many students leaving within their first year without qualifications or completing a whole school term. This issue is one of the most critical problems confronting today's education system, necessitating preemptive measures to combat it head-on. Schools can achieve their goals more effectively while optimizing their budgets by allocating more time and resources to those who most require it. This approach benefits individual students and contributes to a healthier, more productive learning environment.

Individual mentoring and school guidance are pivotal to any effective school tutorial program. These programs are instrumental in helping students acclimate to new environments, understand school rules, and socialize with peers who may be unfamiliar. Furthermore, these systems offer educators valuable insights into how best to cater to individual students' needs, regardless of class size or grade level. This tailored approach is essential in combating the low achievement rates plaguing numerous schools worldwide.

However, a comprehensive approach to education extends beyond academic success. It is incumbent upon schools to focus on the social and cultural aspects of education. The integration of these practices has shown considerable progress in recent years, indicating that we're on the path towards achieving high-quality education standards in contemporary schools.

Artificial intelligence has been heralded as a potential solution to many challenges facing today's education systems. Among its possible applications, AI could reduce the dropout rate in secondary schools by enhancing classroom management and communication with students and parents. It can also provide resources for struggling students and predict which students are at risk of dropping out. By monitoring student performance and behavior, AI can offer real-time insights without constant human surveillance.

The advent of teaching machines brings promise but also invites debate. While some see them as revolutionary tools to aid learning, others fear they may infringe on the role of human teachers and blur ethical boundaries. Teaching labs have explored AI technology's application in education, considering it a potential solution for students who struggle with traditional public school or homeschooling methods. However, this exploration raises several questions.

What role do teaching machines play in reducing school failure? Advocates argue that these technologies can enhance learning and engagement. Conversely, some voice concerns about AI's impact on traditional teaching roles if it becomes widely accepted as a replacement for human educators or assistants. As we navigate this new frontier in education, teachers, parents, and students must remain informed and engaged in conversation. The objective should always be to leverage technology to enhance teaching, not to replace the irreplaceable human touch.

Teachers, parents, and students must recognize the potential pitfalls of integrating artificial intelligence in education. Questions arise regarding its influence on traditional teaching methods; for instance, can a machine provide the same level of care and attention as a human teacher? How will governments ensure that students continue receiving quality education amidst such technological advancements?

According to the United Nations Educational, Scientific and Cultural Organization (UNESCO), the number of children denied access to education has increased by a million since 2016, reaching 264 million.[91] As the world becomes increasingly technologically advanced, it is crucial to ensure these advancements, such as AI, are deployed effectively and responsibly within the educational sector.

In recent decades, we have seen a surge in the use of mechanical devices in classrooms. Interactive whiteboards and computers, for example, offer interactive activities during lessons, aiming to keep children engaged without constant human intervention. However, it is important to note that successful implementation requires careful oversight to ensure these devices function correctly.

Several countries have enacted government policies to improve school performance and quality of life, such as the No Child Left Behind (NCLB) Act in the United States and the European Programme for International Student Assessment (PISA).[92] However, these policies often overlook that not all students possess the same academic capabilities, and some might struggle to meet the set requirements.

Hence, if governments aim to reduce dropout rates, they must consider providing schools with additional funding and resources to support struggling students. Improved classroom management and enhanced communication between teachers, parents, and educators are also essential. Community education initiatives, for instance, could encourage parents to enroll their children in school, reduce the number of out-of-school children, and even provide financial stability for families.

One way to help students succeed in the classroom is through complimentary breakfast and lunch programs. These initiatives alleviate hunger, reduce absences, and enhance classroom performance. Early child development programs can also be beneficial, preparing

---

[91]. "UNESCO: 264 million children do not go to school" 2017, (https://www.dw.com/en/unesco-264-million-children-dont-go-to-school/a-41084932).

[92]. American University, "5 Ways Policy Makers Can Improve the Quality of Education" 2019, (https://soeonline.american.edu/blog/5-ways-policy-makers-can-improve-the-quality-of-education).

children for school and helping them develop essential skills such as communication and technology utilization.

Integrating AI in education seeks to build on these strengths and cater to students' interests, goals, and progress. The competitive advantage of AI lies in its ability to provide personalized tutoring, which is beneficial for students struggling with subjects like English or math. Universities worldwide are leveraging AI to enhance their teaching efficacy, fostering a more profound understanding of human learning among their students. As we progress, we must continue exploring these opportunities while remaining mindful of potential challenges.

How we can help students focus

The ability to focus is an increasing asset in our fast-paced, tech-centric world. Amid a cacophony of distractions, ranging from the constant hum of car horns to the relentless stream of phone notifications, a moment of quiet contemplation can seem like an impossible challenge. However, fostering a haven for one's thoughts away from the hustle and bustle of daily life can offer profound benefits.

For students, honing the ability to concentrate is an investment in their future. This skill enables individuals to rise above the constant noise of everyday life, allowing them to zero in on what truly matters. Whether it is academic work, hobbies, or personal introspection, maintaining focus can significantly enhance performance and help students reach their goals. Moreover, it is a potent tool for relaxation, providing an escape from daily stresses and offering moments of tranquil silence.

However, the art of focusing is not inherent; it is a skill that requires cultivation. While some people may naturally excel at concentrating on multiple tasks simultaneously, others may struggle to focus on a single task. Those interested in enhancing their concentration abilities should begin by training their attention span and committing to one task at a time without succumbing to distractions. As their focus strengthens, they can gradually tackle more complex tasks.

It is important to remember that everyone can improve their focus, even if they were not born with a natural aptitude for it. Like any other skill, the ability to focus can be developed and refined through practice. The more we exercise this mental muscle, the stronger and more efficient it becomes, ultimately enabling us to navigate our noisy world with greater ease and productivity.

In this fast-paced, modern world, taking the time for introspection and self-reflection is more critical than ever. Amidst our bustling lives, we often overlook opportunities for self-analysis, which can lead to feelings of frustration and, in some cases, depression. However, cultivating an internal focus—conducting an intimate inquiry into oneself—can yield significant benefits.

An internal focus involves thoroughly examining one's thoughts, emotions, and motivations before deciding. This introspective journey typically increases self-awareness and promotes more efficient and effective decision-making processes.

For students, maintaining focus amidst numerous distractions can be a daunting task. Still, setting aside time for introspection can prove beneficial. It allows students to connect with their identities and desires more deeply. Decisions made from a place of self-awareness are far more effective than those based purely on instinct. Thus, learning to focus inward is a valuable skill that can serve students well throughout their lives.

The process of self-analysis is a fascinating journey I have personally undertaken and sought to instill in my students. It involves delving into your thoughts and emotions and observing how they fluctuate over different life stages, from childhood to adulthood. Our minds generate many ideas—some, from primitive brain regions, are more spontaneous and less controllable, like emotions or anger. Others, originating from more developed areas, are more logical, deductive, and controllable. Recognizing that we do not control all thoughts equally can help us understand why certain things can easily distract us.

Reflecting on our evolution as humans and the development of our brains over time is captivating. The ability to focus on internal thoughts and feelings rather than merely reacting to external stimuli represents a significant advancement in human consciousness. This level of self-awareness is a valuable asset in various life areas. By better understanding our emotional responses and reactions to different situations, we gain invaluable insight—an advantage in our digital age.

One of my concerns is the tendency to overload ourselves with commitments, often unnecessary, which can erode our concentration. We must learn to prioritize and say no to some engagements to maintain a balanced schedule. To me, focus is not just about concentrating on one thing—it is also about consciously ignoring distractions. Essentially, it is about discerning what matters most and less. Learning to prioritize effectively is fundamental to maintaining focus and achieving our goals.

In today's fast-paced world, the ability to focus has become a rarity. The constant pressure to multitask leaves students overwhelmed and distracted, making it difficult for them to complete tasks efficiently. With the rise of artificial intelligence and algorithms capable of handling multiple tasks simultaneously, one might wonder: how can we improve our ability to concentrate in an era of relentless distractions?

To enhance focus, we must instill awareness in our students about their surroundings and the importance of effective time management. We can help students channel their energies more productively by assigning specific tasks instead of promoting multitasking. Implementing these strategies could lead to noticeable improvements in student focus and motivation.

Motivation can be further boosted through three fundamental approaches: fostering a sense of mastery, integrating playfulness into learning, and encouraging diversity in the classroom. The satisfaction of their accomplishments drives students to pursue further education. Incorporating an element of fun into educational activities enhances engagement while promoting diversity and making all students feel included and valued, fostering a conducive learning environment.

A concern that often arises is the growing lack of attention people generally pay to others' conversations, indicating a loss of focus on interpersonal interactions and experiential learning. This trend could result in missed opportunities for personal growth and understanding. Conversely, attentive people tend to have greater control over their thoughts, leading to a deeper comprehension of themselves and the world around them.

Lastly, let us prioritize teaching students how to initiate tasks and devise effective plans. This approach will guide them through the three stages of learning: acquisition, application, and reflection/evaluation. By mastering these steps, students can maximize their learning potential and develop skills that will serve them well beyond the classroom.

How we can help students gain maturity

In our contemporary society, the underlying notion is that maturity diminishes one's value. This sentiment seems prevalent among recent generations—those who have grown up in an era marked by significant technological advancements. These advancements, while undeniably making our lives easier and more accessible, may inadvertently contribute to a prolonged sense of infancy stretching into adulthood. But at what cost does this occur? This phenomenon suggests a potential inability to fully embrace adulthood, creating a state of extended infancy that belies the societal benchmarks traditionally associated with "adulthood."

Defining what it means to be an adult is crucial to comprehending this trend entirely. Typically, adulthood is legally defined as reaching the age of majority, which in most areas is eighteen. Upon reaching this age, individuals are granted the full spectrum of rights and responsibilities associated with adulthood. The transition from adolescence to adulthood is a legal milestone and a significant life transition involving emotional, cognitive, and social changes.

However, societal and technological shifts may blur these traditional milestones, leading to a sense of prolonged adolescence or delayed adulthood. As we navigate these complex dynamics, promoting a balanced perspective on maturity is essential. Rather than viewing it as a loss of value, we should celebrate it as a stage of life rich with growth, independence, and new opportunities.

In times past, reaching the age of majority was widely regarded as a significant rite of passage, marking the transition into adulthood. It ushered in an era where young individuals were given greater responsibilities and expected to make meaningful contributions to society. However, today's landscape paints a starkly different picture. An increasing number of individuals appear hesitant to shed the cloak of their childhood and step into adulthood, opting to extend their youth for as long as possible.

Several factors fuel this trend, including the mounting pressure young people face to succeed. In an era characterized by escalating living expenses and diminishing job security, the fear of failure looms large among the youth. There are numerous reasons why people may resist maturing, which only serves to increase this anxiety.

One such reason is the daunting prospect of assuming more responsibilities at home and work that comes with aging. The mere thought of this can be overwhelming for many. Another deterrent is the fear of change. With age comes inevitable physical transformations, a stark reminder of our mortality. Additionally, individuals might have to navigate personal life changes, such as relationship upheavals or losing a loved one, which can intensify the reluctance to grow up.

Growing up is an inevitable, natural, and necessary part of life. Educators and caregivers can guide students on this journey into adulthood by continuously providing valuable information and resources. These tools will help them understand what it means to be an adult and underscore the importance of embracing maturity.

Continued education is a pivotal part of this process. Focusing on societal interactions and personal relationships and sharing stories from diverse perspectives can give students a broader understanding of adult life. Additionally, offering resources on practical aspects like financial planning and career development can equip them with skills they will need in the future.

Furthermore, support systems such as counseling and mentorship programs can prove invaluable. These services can help students navigate the multifaceted challenges associated with adulthood, ultimately leading to happier, more fulfilling lives.

One effective strategy to bolster self-esteem among young people is to illustrate how adults manage daily challenges. While premature exposure to adult responsibilities may lead to regret later in life, providing constructive tools and strategies can better prepare them for growing up.

Maturity plays a crucial role in learning and acquiring new skills. In my experience, students who exhibit maturity often excel in their endeavors, achieving results faster. This maturity can significantly impact their future success if nurtured appropriately.

Lastly, it is essential to acknowledge that some individuals may struggle with accepting the aging process, possibly due to fear or denial. Regardless of these feelings, it is vital to remember that growing older is a natural part of life. There is no shame in aging, and embracing adulthood can be a rewarding experience, paving the way for a happier, more fulfilled life.

CHAPTER 6

Artificial Intelligence in Special Education

Could artificial intelligence serve as a valuable tool for individuals with special needs? Considering the recent advancements in AI, it is hard to envision a demographic that this revolutionary technology has not touched. Yet, the full potential of AI in enhancing the lives of those with special needs remains largely unexplored.

Artificial intelligence has already begun to demonstrate its potential in aiding individuals with special needs, particularly in their interaction with contemporary technological devices. For instance, it has proven invaluable for people with visual impairments, auditory challenges, or mobility restrictions due to illness or injury.[93] Artificial intelligence facilitates efficient communication, allowing these individuals to interact seamlessly with the world around them. Moreover, those on the autism spectrum or individuals suffering from traumatic brain injuries, such as stroke victims experiencing locked-in syndrome, can communicate more effectively through technology tailored to their needs. It offers many exciting applications, including

---

[93]. Snow, J., "People with Disabilities Are Using AI to Improve Their Lives" 2019, (https://www.pbs.org/wgbh/nova/article/people-with-disabilities-use-ai-to-improve-their-lives/?msclkid=8e744bd4a87811ec93c08d26ab07082).

image recognition and voice recognition software, which can be leveraged to assist individuals with special needs. These innovative solutions transform our lives, offering newfound independence and opportunities to those who may have previously felt marginalized.

For instance, AI has assisted those with hearing impairments and other disabilities that impede speech. Innovative solutions include text-to-speech software, sign language translation applications, and even devices that transmit vibrations to aid communication when speaking becomes challenging. Such technologies enable individuals to express themselves more effectively, making conversations more accessible and inclusive.

In the realm of education, AI is already making a significant difference. It is enhancing learning experiences for people with disabilities, offering services like reading aloud schoolbooks for visually impaired individuals, and providing audiobooks for those who are illiterate or have hearing impairments.

Looking ahead, the role of AI in supporting people with various disabilities promises to expand. It could, for example, detect nonverbal cues and pauses in speech to determine if someone needs assistance. As a society, we advocate for those who may not have a voice or the necessary resources. The future of AI holds immense potential for bridging these gaps and facilitating a more inclusive world where everyone can thrive.

Hearing impairments

Artificial intelligence is proving to be a game changer in improving accessibility for individuals with special needs, particularly those with hearing impairments. Several innovative applications of AI have emerged in recent years, significantly enhancing communication and interaction capabilities for these individuals.[94]

---

94. Utermohlen K., "4 Applications of Artificial Intelligence for Hearing Loss" 2018, (https://medium.com/@karl.utermohlen/4-applications-of-artificial-intelligence-for-hearing-loss-64f3e189847e).

One notable application of AI is personalizing closed captioning, assisting in auditory tasks, and isolating sounds for more transparent comprehension. Moreover, AI-powered devices such as Microsoft Translator, Automated Speech Recognition technology, SignAll, KinTrans, Ava mobile app, and Google sign language software are also making significant strides in aiding people with hearing impairments.[95]

Furthermore, AI is being incorporated into hearing aids to identify and diminish background noise, improving the quality of sound individuals perceive.[96] Language prediction and lip-reading, powered by AI and Natural Language Processing (NLP), have also been leveraged to ease the lives of the hearing impaired.[97] Several apps, like Ava and Google Live Transcribe, use AI to transcribe group conversations, making communication more accessible for those with hearing impairments.[98] In addition, partnerships between tech giants like Google and Cochlear and academic and hearing leaders are paving the way for more personalized AI hearing technology.[99]

These advancements underline the transformative potential of AI in enhancing the quality of life for people with special needs. As we continue to explore and harness this potential, it is important to ensure that these technologies are accessible and inclusive, empowering all individuals to communicate effectively and efficiently navigate their environments.

---

[95]. IndustryWired. "Top 7 AI Tools to Battle Against Hearing Impairment" 2021, (https://industrywired.com/top-7-ai-tools-to-battle-against-hearing-impairment/).

[96]. Burry M., "Hearing aids with Artificial Intelligence" 2021, (https://www.healthyhearing.com/report/53168-Hearing-aids-artificial-intelligence-deep-learning-oticon).

[97]. Asokan A. "5 Ways in Which AI Is Improving Accessibility for the Hearing Impairment" 2019, (https://analyticsindiamag.com/5-ways-in-which-ai-is-improving-accessibility-for-the-hearing-impaired/).

[98]. Department of Human Services Minnesota, "Apps for Hearing Loss" (https://mn.gov/deaf-hard-of-hearing/assistive-technology/apps/).

[99]. Chung G., "Five New Partnerships to Shape the Future of Hearing Technology" 2023, (https://blog.google/intl/en-au/company-news/technology/ai-hearing-initiative/).

Visual impairments

Imagine a world where individuals with disabilities enjoy equal opportunities to contribute as productive members of society. What if technology could enable blind people to read books, prepare meals, or even perceive the faces of their loved ones? Artificial intelligence has the potential to do all this and more, empowering those with special needs to lead more independent lives.

Blind individuals traditionally rely on their other senses to compensate for their lack of sight. Artificial intelligence can augment this by vocally identifying and interpreting sounds in the environment and providing precise information about surrounding activities. This technology can enhance what some visually impaired individuals describe as "seeing through their ears" by using sound and frequency to gauge the proximity of obstacles. AI advancements are poised to create auditory alerts, enabling individuals to react appropriately to someone approaching from any direction. Consider the transformative impact of a blind person independently using navigation services, trained by an individual who can interpret the visual intricacies of different streets at various times of the day or night.

AI's role is not limited to aiding the visually impaired. It is already making strides in assistive technologies for older adults, such as intelligent hearing aids that automatically adjust based on location or noise levels. Future applications could even involve scanning images from books and converting them into audio files, making them accessible to those unable to see them.

It has also been employed to develop applications enabling people with disabilities to use cell phones without audio capabilities. Achieving this involves detecting hand or head movements and converting them into on-screen clicks. Such technology can significantly improve educational outcomes for students with disabilities, allowing teachers to better understand and implement individualized learning plans.

In addition, AI is being used as a translator for individuals with hearing impairments who do not speak English or another language. The next frontier could include AI-powered devices that translate tactile braille data into spoken words, enabling blind individuals to audibly perceive what they are reading.

Consider innovations like the Voicebox from the University College London Interaction Lab, which converts speech into text, or Google Lens, which recognizes objects and provides relevant information through a camera lens system.[100,101] These technologies are transforming how individuals with special needs interact with the world.

Artificial intelligence holds tremendous potential for assisting people with special needs, such as blindness, by providing them with a voice and helping them find information or navigate their surroundings. This promotes independence, which is crucial for mental health and safety, and enriches their educational experiences. As AI continues to evolve, its role in enhancing the lives of individuals with special needs will undoubtedly expand, paving the way for a more inclusive future.

---

[100]. Research Impact, "Voicebox: Facilitating Science Teaching in Schools" 2014, (https://www.ucl.ac.uk/impact/case-studies/2014/dec/voicebox-facilitating-science-teaching-schools).

[101]. JR Raphael, "16 Ways Google Lens Can Make You More Productive on Android" Computerworld, 2023, (https://www.computerworld.com/article/3572639/google-lens.html).

CHAPTER 7

Artificial Intelligence Can Do Everything Regarding Education Without Humans

Artificial intelligence is revolutionizing education, enabling new forms of interaction, and enhancing human capacities. It allows students and teachers to engage in more natural modes of communication, such as speaking, gesturing, and sketching.[102]

AI's deployment in education aims to bolster human abilities and protect human values.[103] It transforms teaching and learning practices, with AI language models serving as practice tools for novice teachers.[104] Furthermore, AI can significantly enhance student learning outcomes when paired with high-quality learning materials and instruction.

---

[102]. Artificial Intelligence - Office of Educational Technology (https://tech.ed.gov/ai/).

[103]. "Artificial Intelligence in Education" (https://www.unesco.org/en/digital-education/artificial-intelligence).

[104]. Chen C., "AI Will Transform Teaching and Learning. Let's Get It Right" 2023, (https://hai.stanford.edu/news/ai-will-transform-teaching-and-learning-lets-get-it-right).

The International Journal of Artificial Intelligence in Education publishes research concerning the application of AI in education.[105] AI applications in education are vast, including plagiarism detection, exam integrity monitoring, chatbots for enrollment and retention, and transcription services.[106]

However, banning AI in schools could potentially reinforce digital inequities and widen the digital divide.[107] Artificial intelligence is a critical element of any STEM curriculum, with adaptive software already making its way into classrooms.[108]

The use of AI in US education is expected to grow by 47.5% from 2017 to 2021. Chris Dede, a professor at Harvard Graduate School of Education, discusses how education can evolve to work with—rather than fight against—artificial intelligence.[109]

Artificial intelligence can automate many time-consuming administrative tasks in teaching and learning, such as grading assignments, providing feedback on student work, or even detecting plagiarism. Machine learning algorithms and natural language processing can help teachers quickly identify patterns in student performance. Personalized learning, plagiarism detection, and 24-7 tutoring access are examples of how AI enhances the classroom experience for students and teachers.

In conclusion, AI's integration into education holds significant potential for improving teaching and learning experiences, fostering

---

[105]. International Journal of Artificial Intelligence in Education, 2023, (https://www.springer.com/journal/40593).

[106]. University of San Diego, "43 Examples of Artificial Intelligence in Education" (https://onlinedegrees.sandiego.edu/artificial-intelligence-education/).

[107]. Phillips V., "Intelligent Classrooms: What AI Means for the Future of Education" 2023, (https://www.forbes.com/sites/vickiphillips/2023/06/07/intelligent-classrooms-what-ai-means-for-the-future-of-education/).

[108]. "AI Exploration for Educators: Putting Educators and Students in the Driver's Seat" (https://www.iste.org/areas-of-focus/AI-in-education).

[109]. Anderson J., Harvard EdCast "Educating in a World of Artificial Intelligence" 2023, (https://www.gse.harvard.edu/ideas/edcast/23/02/harvard-edcast-educating-world-artificial-intelligence).

personalized learning, and promoting efficiency in administrative tasks.

The relevance of human intelligence in AI-powered education

Artificial intelligence has undeniably revolutionized numerous aspects of our lives. Still, it is crucial to remember that it fundamentally relies on human creativity and intelligence for accurate interpretation and direction. While AI can effectively predict our online behavior or the likelihood of traffic violations, it lacks the unique perspective necessary to match or surpass human common sense and intuition.

Here are three key reasons that underscore why AI cannot operate without human intervention.

- *Data annotation.* AI systems are designed to process millions, if not billions, of random data points. However, they cannot function independently without the guidance of an AI programmer. The AI algorithm refines its understanding by tracking and correcting false assumptions through data annotation. This involves semantics, categorization, and other details within images, videos, and text.
- *Oversight.* Effective planning within and beyond the digital framework requires proper management of inputs, outputs, and other processes. This structure is integral to the functionality and utility of artificial intelligence. For example, automatic processing systems can fail when a web form changes, especially if engineers have not updated the logic or data to accommodate the changes. Maintaining coordinated AI systems requires human intervention to actively prevent such failures by updating the algorithms and data when forms or interfaces evolve. Moreover, without human oversight, lapses in AI performance could go unnoticed for extended periods, disrupting productivity.

- *Data management.* Machine learning algorithms excel at recognizing text, video, and sound, each of which demands exceptional management. One of the significant challenges in the widespread adoption of AI for task automation is curating effective data points. Many algorithms can successfully employ transfer learning techniques, reducing the need for regular discrete data that enhances the predictive ability of the algorithm. However, deciding on the data points for the transfer requires a meticulous selection process and human intelligence on the subject.

In conclusion, while AI has made significant strides in various fields, its effective functioning still heavily relies on human intelligence and intervention. From data annotation and oversight to data management, humans are crucial to ensuring AI's accuracy and efficiency. As we continue to push the boundaries of AI capabilities, this symbiotic relationship between AI and human intelligence will remain at the core of its success.

Real-world application of AI in education

While it is evident that artificial intelligence has the potential to replace human teachers in the educational system, that is not the ultimate goal. Instead, we envision a symbiotic educational design where AI automates repetitive tasks, compensates for human limitations, and enhances learning and teaching experiences.

To illustrate this concept, let us consider some real-world applications of AI:

- *External support and tutoring.* Every parent who has struggled with helping their child with homework can appreciate the value of after-school support. Students often encounter challenges outside the classroom that can impact their academic performance. Artificial intelligence can provide personalized study programs and tutoring outside school hours, catering to various learning styles. As more AI-based educational applications—like AI mentors for students, virtual global conferencing for teachers, and intelligent content—are developed, the benefits of AI in education will continue to unfold, albeit at a slower pace than in other sectors.

- *Increased accessibility for learners.* AI tools can facilitate global classrooms, accommodating a broader audience, including those with impairments or non-native English speakers. For instance, many software applications and plug-ins can translate spoken words into real-time subtitles, aiding students in following lessons and opening educational opportunities for learners who are out of school or require different learning levels.

- *Collaboration between teachers and AI.* AI is leveraged to develop educational tools for testing systems and skill acquisition. As AI educational systems mature, they offer teachers and schools the opportunity to enhance their effectiveness. Its role extends beyond personalization and efficiency. It also streamlines administrative tasks, freeing up teachers' time for adaptability and more profound understanding—areas where AI might fall short.

- *Automating administrative tasks.* Teachers often spend considerable time grading tests, homework, and classwork. Artificial intelligence can expedite these tasks while providing individualized recommendations to address learning gaps. Machines excel at grading multiple-choice tests and are not far from assessing written answers. By taking over administrative duties, AI allows teachers to focus more on students and enhance learning experiences.

- *Differentiated and individualized learning.* The education sector has long prioritized adjusting learning systems to cater to individual student needs. However, managing this differentiation can overwhelm teachers, especially when handling large classes. Various companies have developed AI solutions to address this issue, creating platforms that use AI for learning, assessment, and feedback for students from pre-kindergarten to college.

These tools will keep getting better, and soon, AI will be able to look at students' personalities to see which ones are having trouble understanding lessons. This way, the teacher can change the class pace and level of difficulty to fit each student. While personalizing the curriculum for each student may seem ambitious now, the continuous development of AI-based solutions brings us closer to this reality.

In conclusion, an ideal educational system seamlessly integrates the best attributes of teachers and AI, working symbiotically to benefit students everywhere. Given the pervasive role of AI in our future, students must be exposed to technology from an early age.

Myths surrounding the involvement of AI in education

Incorporating artificial intelligence into the realm of education brings with it a plethora of benefits. However, some downsides have led to the creation of certain myths over time. A lack of comprehensive understanding of this technology has resulted in people clinging to misconceptions. Some of the most common erroneous beliefs include:

1. Artificial intelligence will surpass human intelligence.

Many believe these systems will become more proficient as we invest more time and effort into developing AI. While there's truth to the idea that AI capabilities are expanding, it has led to the widespread notion that AI will eventually achieve human-level intelligence. Evidence has indicated that AI can exceed average human intelligence in specific tasks. However, this does not provide a complete picture.

It is essential to understand that while AI can accomplish specific tasks more efficiently than humans, it does not possess the breadth of human cognitive abilities. Artificial intelligence excels at pattern recognition and data processing but falls short in creative thinking, empathy, and understanding nuanced contexts—areas where human intelligence shines.

Therefore, while AI continues to evolve and improve, the belief that it will surpass human intelligence is, for now, more of a myth than a reality. As we progress into the age of AI, it is important to dispel such misconceptions and foster a more informed understanding of what AI can and cannot do.

2. Artificial intelligence and machine learning are the same things.

Artificial intelligence and machine learning (ML) are often used interchangeably, leading to the misconception that they are the same. Although closely related, these two concepts are distinct and independent entities.

Artificial intelligence refers to machines or software mimicking human intelligence, learning from algorithms and datasets programmed into their systems. However, it is not entirely autonomous and still requires a degree of human intervention for tasks such as programming and decision-making.

On the other hand, machine learning, a subset of AI, involves using self-learning algorithms that improve over time with increased exposure to data without being explicitly programmed to do so. These programs, also known as offline learning algorithms, play a crucial role in advancing AI technology by enabling it to learn and adapt autonomously.

In essence, while machine learning and AI are intertwined, each serves a unique function in advanced computing. Understanding their roles and interactions is key to effectively leveraging their capabilities.

3. Machines will be autonomous.

The concept of machines achieving full autonomy is common in discussions surrounding artificial intelligence. However, the notion that AI or machines will become independent is somewhat misguided.

It is crucial to remember that AI systems are not self-generating entities. Human developers play a pivotal role in meticulously designing and programming them, shaping their functionality. For instance, these programmers write codes that dictate how AI should operate.

Moreover, machine learning, a subset of AI, operates based on algorithms, which serve as the decision-making core of AI. These algorithms can be fine-tuned to process specific data while ignoring others. This implies that AI systems strictly follow the constraints set by their programming and act in accordance with the data they receive.

In principle, while AI can perform remarkable feats, its operations are ultimately governed by human intervention and oversight. The idea of machines running independently amok, therefore, leans more toward the realm of science fiction than reality. As we continue to advance in AI, it is essential to maintain an informed perspective, understanding the capabilities of these technologies and their inherent limitations.

4. Artificial intelligence could jeopardize confidentiality.

Unifying artificial intelligence into various systems has undeniably raised concerns about privacy and confidentiality, especially in sensitive environments such as classrooms. However, it is important to dispel the misconception that introducing AI tools like chatbots automatically compromises privacy.

While it is true that many digital systems are designed to track and harvest data, this does not necessarily apply to all AI implementations. AI tools, including chatbots, can be specifically programmed to respect user privacy.

For instance, developers can design chatbots to avoid storing unnecessary data or requesting personal details from students. They can also ensure these AI tools adhere strictly to privacy laws and guidelines. Students can interact with these chatbots without fear of mishandling their personal information.

While privacy concerns are valid in the age of AI, it is vital to understand that AI doesn't inherently jeopardize confidentiality. With the proper programming and ethical considerations, AI can be a valuable tool in the education sector without compromising students' privacy.

5. AI will predict human behavior flawlessly.

The notion that artificial intelligence can flawlessly predict human behavior is a widely held misconception. While it seems like a favorable perspective on the capabilities of AI, it does not accurately reflect reality.

Humans, by nature, are complex and unpredictable. Despite advancements in AI technology, it remains challenging for these systems to anticipate human behavior fully. AI relies on a steady stream of current data points to achieve a certain level of accuracy. However, even with the most up-to-date data, expecting perfect predictions from these systems is unrealistic.

That said, the power of AI lies in its ongoing learning and adaptability. As we continue to develop and utilize AI, it becomes more knowledgeable, gradually improving its ability to answer questions and predict behaviors. Each human interaction provides new data for analysis, enhancing AI's predictive capabilities over time.

In summary, the more we engage with AI, the better it becomes at understanding and predicting our behaviors. However, while its proficiency may increase, it is important to remember that flawless prediction of human behavior remains beyond the current scope of AI. Thus, we should appreciate AI for what it can do—enhance our lives through machine learning and data analysis—rather than expecting it to mirror human cognition perfectly.

6. AI embodies objectivity.

The concept that artificial intelligence is inherently objective is a common misunderstanding. Human input, rules, and data programming heavily influence artificial intelligence systems. Given that humans are naturally predisposed to biases, AI, as a product of human creation, may also reflect these biases.

For example, AI systems regularly retrained with data from sources like social media can be susceptible to negative influences and unchecked biases. This is because these platforms often echo the prejudices and biases present in society.

The challenge with objectivity in AI is that bias cannot be entirely eradicated. Striving to eliminate bias is, paradoxically, another form of bias. It presents us with a complex problem that does not have a straightforward solution.

However, there are measures we can take to mitigate the impact of bias on AI. One practical approach is to minimize human interference in AI processes and utilize unique datasets that offer a wider variety of perspectives. Additionally, having diverse teams working on AI algorithms can help check and balance biases, leading to more impartial and fair AI systems.

While AI may not embody perfect objectivity, we can take preventive steps to ensure its decision-making processes are fair and unbiased.

7. AI understands everything.

The notion that artificial intelligence understands everything is a common misconception. While AI has made tremendous strides in various fields, it must remember that its knowledge and intelligence are limited to the data it has been fed and the experiences it has acquired through human interaction.

For instance, many people may wonder why the virtual assistant on their phones does not seem as smart as the ones portrayed on television. The answer lies in the datasets used to train these AI systems.

These virtual assistants can only understand and respond based on the information they have been programmed with.

This limitation becomes evident when AI encounters unfamiliar elements, such as typographical errors or colloquial terms outside its vocabulary. Artificial intelligence may not perform as expected in such scenarios, leading to potential misunderstandings or inaccuracies.

Artificial intelligence has dramatically enhanced our technological capabilities, but it is not all-knowing. The quality and breadth of the data it has been trained on determines its understanding and performance. As we continue to refine and expand these datasets, we can expect AI to become increasingly proficient and adaptable.

CHAPTER 8

AI Agents

Artificial intelligence is continually evolving, and one of the most recent advancements is AI agents' capacity to share knowledge. This ability transforms machine learning, allowing AI agents to learn a broader range of tasks more quickly.[110]

A study conducted at the University of Southern California's Viterbi School of Engineering revealed that robots could learn from each other like humans do.[111] This process of mutual learning among AI agents is facilitated through a technique known as Shared Knowledge Lifelong Learning (SKILL), which involves several independent learning agents sequentially acquiring new skills.[112]

Knowledge sharing in AI is not restricted to the realm of robotics. AI also enhances decision-making processes by allowing machines to

---

[110]. Hardesty G., "AI That Teaches Other AI" 2023, (https://viterbischool.usc.edu/news/2023/07/teaching-robots-to-teach-other-robots/).

[111]. Sweezy T., "AI Study Finds Robots Can Learn From Each Other Just Like Humans" 2023, (https://hothardware.com/news/ai-study-finds-robots-learn-from-each-other).

[112]. Bild N., "AI Goes Back to School" 2023, (https://www.hackster.io/news/ai-goes-back-to-school-828d17db7c45).

acquire, process, and use knowledge.[113] This capability is instrumental in knowledge management, where AI can automate and augment the knowledge creation process by extracting insights from various sources. However, knowledge sharing among AI agents is not without its challenges. One of the key hurdles is overcoming silos to connect disparate people with the practices and knowledge they need.[114]

Despite these challenges, shared learning involves individuals working together and exchanging knowledge and insights, which has yielded remarkable results.[115]

Moreover, research shows that AI, like humans, retains information better when faced with diverse tasks than those sharing similar features. This finding is significant as it helps overcome "catastrophic forgetting," a common problem in AI where an AI system forgets previously learned information when new information is introduced.[116]

To conclude, the ability of AI agents to share knowledge is revolutionizing machine learning. We can expect more efficient and versatile AI systems by enabling AI agents to learn from each other.

---

[113]. Rhem A., "The Connection between Artificial Intelligence and Knowledge Management" 2017, (https://www.kminstitute.org/blog/connection-between-artificial-intelligence-and-knowledge-management).

[114]. Jarrahi M., Askay D., Eshraghi A., and Smith P., "Artificial Intelligence and Knowledge Management: A Partnership Between Human and AI" 2022, (https://www.sciencedirect.com/science/article/pii/S0007681322000222).

[115]. Çitak E., "Collaboration Sparks the Flames of Machine Learning" 2023, (https://dataconomy.com/2023/07/17/shared-learning-peer-to-peer-learning/).

[116]. Woodall T., "Overcoming 'Catastrophic Forgetting': A Leap in AI Continuous Learning" Neuroscience News, 2023, (https://neurosciencenews.com/ai-continuous-learning-23671/).

CHAPTER 9

Artificial Intelligence and Ethics in Education

The incorporation of artificial intelligence into education is a topic that has been garnering significant attention recently. As AI continues to evolve and become more sophisticated, it is increasingly being integrated into various aspects of our lives, including education. However, this integration raises several ethical considerations.

The first concern relates to data privacy. AI systems often require access to vast amounts of personal data to function effectively. This data can include students' academic records, behavioral patterns, and sometimes even biometric information. There is a risk that this data could be misused or mishandled, leading to privacy breaches.

Secondly, there is the issue of fairness. AI systems are only as unbiased as the data they are trained on. If the underlying data reflects societal biases, the AI system could inadvertently perpetuate these biases, leading to unfair outcomes. For example, an AI system might favor students from certain backgrounds over others, creating an inequitable learning environment.

Another ethical concern is the potential replacement of human teachers by AI. While AI can automate certain aspects of teaching, it cannot replicate a teacher's emotional support, mentorship, or human connection. There is a fear that an over-reliance on AI could devalue these essential human elements of education.

Finally, there is the question of accountability. Who is responsible if an AI system makes a mistake, such as incorrectly grading a student or misdiagnosing a learning difficulty? The lack of clear-cut accountability in AI decision-making poses a significant ethical challenge.

Navigating ethical challenges

Addressing these ethical concerns requires a multipronged approach. Firstly, stringent data protection measures must be implemented to ensure student data is handled securely and confidentially. Secondly, steps must be taken to ensure that AI systems are trained on diverse and representative datasets to minimize bias.

Furthermore, clear guidelines should be established outlining the role of AI in the classroom. Artificial intelligence should be used to enhance and not replace human teaching. Teachers should remain at the center of the educational process, with AI serving as a supportive tool.

Lastly, legal and regulatory frameworks need to be developed to address the issue of accountability in AI decision-making. These frameworks should clearly define who is responsible when an AI system makes a mistake and outline the recourse available to those affected.

While the use of AI in education holds immense potential, it is crucial to navigate the associated ethical challenges carefully. By doing so, we can harness the benefits of AI in education while safeguarding the rights and interests of students.

The precision of AI in diagnosing learner interactions within AI in Education (AIED) systems is a central concern for the community. Simultaneously, while AI could potentially compromise academic integrity, it also offers opportunities by improving users' abilities. Thus, it becomes essential to guide students and educators about the benefits and limitations of AI tools, promote their ethical use, and maintain academic integrity.

Artificial intelligence carries immense potential to enrich education, but its ethical implications warrant careful consideration. As AI progresses, it is imperative to set rules for its use in education, ensuring respect for privacy, promoting fairness, and preserving academic integrity.

Significant societal implications arise from the evolution of our education system, especially from elementary to university-level training. With the growing integration of AI into educational contexts, there is a concern that an emphasis on technical proficiency might overshadow the cultivation of creativity and flexible thinking.

These skills are crucial for tackling complex challenges ranging from climate change mitigation to developing innovative technologies in emerging sectors like renewable energy. However, an education system heavily dependent on AI may unintentionally prioritize algorithmic thinking over these vital skills.

This shift raises the question of whether we inadvertently "robotize" our students, fostering more computerlike thinking than creative problem-solving. While computers can perform tasks such as mathematical calculations exponentially faster than humans, it does not guarantee improved student learning outcomes.

There are divergent views on whether AI accelerates learning or has the potential to replace human teachers entirely. As policymakers worldwide tackle the ethical implications of AI in education, further exploration and clarity are required, particularly in establishing ethical boundaries.

Educators leverage this opportunity to create innovative projects exploring the interplay between humans and machines. These initiatives prompt students to scrutinize ethical dilemmas in increasingly data-driven, AI-influenced decision-making environments. Cultivating critical thinking prepares students to navigate a future characterized by extensive automation and digitization.

Research into AI and ethics in education is expanding as educators increasingly utilize AI as a teaching tool. For example, machine learning techniques, such as natural language processing algorithms, analyze student data to form "predictive models" of student performance. This data informs personalized instructional plans. While this approach has effectively increased retention rates, doubts persist regarding its teaching capabilities beyond subjects like literacy and math.

The intersection of AI, ethics, and education is complex and raises a pressing question: should we allow this technology to lead student learning? Many parents might hesitate to entrust their children's education to an algorithm susceptible to becoming outdated or influenced by external factors like advertisers. Parental involvement remains vital amid the ongoing skepticism toward AI-led education.

Ethical concerns emerge when contemplating the idea of humans ceding learning control to AI. There is a widespread fear that corporations could promote content serving their interests, potentially compromising education quality and objectivity if we lose control over what our children learn.

Ethical considerations also extend to how educators implement AI. For instance, if schools offer online tutoring services via chatbots, does this mean they are abdicating their teacher responsibilities?

While AI offers significant opportunities for enhancing education, careful navigation of its implementation is crucial. Considering the ethical implications will ensure a balanced, effective, and responsible approach to teaching and learning.

CHAPTER 10

Which Knowledge Do We Need: Static or Dynamic?

The notion of the "good old days" is prevalent, with many people romanticizing a seemingly more straightforward past. However, it is crucial to remember that every era comes with its challenges, and the good old days may not have been as idyllic as we often perceive them. Therefore, we should avoid glorifying the past and acknowledge that life, in any period, has never been without its difficulties.

In today's fast-paced world, static knowledge—information that remains unchanged over time—is insufficient. While grasping the facts is essential, we must also utilize this knowledge to think critically and uncover truths in our ever-evolving world. The danger of relying solely on static knowledge lies in the potential for complacency; when individuals feel they have sufficiently understood the world, they may cease to learn and explore further.[117]

---

117. Quora, "What is Static General Knowledge?" (https://www.quora.com/What-is-static-general-knowledge?msclkid=af39a04da90511ecaea1edcd381f47c9).

Instead, we must embrace dynamic knowledge, representing information that changes and evolves with discoveries and technological advancements.[118] This knowledge enables us to adapt and grow alongside our rapidly changing environment, keeping us ahead of the curve.

So, how do we discern the truth? How do we best understand the world around us and beyond? Static knowledge plays a role, but it is not enough. We need a dynamic comprehension of all aspects of life and society to overcome our most significant challenges. This is why futurists are vital. They help us anticipate the impact of technological, social, and environmental changes in the future. Understanding how our knowledge will influence society and how we can effectively utilize it is essential.

To cultivate this dynamic understanding in our ever-changing world, we need educators and students eager to step out of their comfort zones, open to new ideas, and willing to take risks in exploring new realms of knowledge.

Knowledge is merely the gateway to critical thinking; exposure to knowledge through education sparks thought. But imagine a world where we were all born with a complete understanding of everything—wouldn't life seem much simpler? Yet, it is essential to recognize that knowledge should serve as a tool for inquiry, not an end in itself.

In an era of readily available information, balancing knowledge acquisition with continuous self-education becomes more crucial than ever. We live in a world abundant with information, yet we often lack the tools to make sense of it. The issue is not a lack of knowledge, but rather that our knowledge tends to be static and fragmented. Thus, embracing dynamic knowledge and continual learning is critical to navigating our information-rich world.

---

[118]. Wikipedia, "Dynamic knowledge repository" (https://en.wikipedia.org/wiki/Dynamic_knowledge_repository).

Augmented cognition

This chapter delves into the transformative potential of augmented cognition in our thinking and learning processes. As individuals, we embrace these innovative ways of perceiving ourselves and the world around us.

Just imagine if embracing these new methodologies enabled us to tap into our past or access comprehensive information about any individual throughout history. How does such unprecedented access to information alter our experience of the world? In what ways might augmented cognition reshape our understanding of ourselves, our environment, and our interactions with those who share it with us?

Integrating augmented cognition into our daily lives promises numerous personal and societal benefits. But what exactly is increased awareness? It is an emerging field in science that explores the implications of humans connecting with digital devices, such as computers and mobile phones.[119] This connectivity's impact on twenty-first century learning and thinking forms a significant part of this research. When connected, humans can share information more swiftly and efficiently than in isolation, theoretically accelerating our learning process by facilitating real-time knowledge sharing.

Significantly, augmented cognition has moved beyond theoretical discourse. Today, numerous devices on the market facilitate faster and more efficient human connection and information sharing. For instance, iPhones come equipped with applications like Siri, enabling users to ask questions and receive answers simply by speaking to their phones. Similarly, Google Glass, a wearable device resembling glasses, features an additional screen on the lens. This allows users to access information or pose queries while observing their immediate surroundings without needing to handle their phones physically.

---

[119]. Wikipedia. "Augmented cognition" (https://en.wikipedia.org/wiki/Augmented_cognition#:~:text=Augmented%20cognition.%20Augmented%20cognition%20is%20an%20interdisciplinary%20area,and%20environments%20where%20human%E2%80%93computer%20interaction%20and%20interfaces%20?msclkid=e917W6a4ca90511ecb715e2eb99193ea9).

To sum up, augmented cognition stands poised to revolutionize our thinking and learning processes. As we navigate this brave new world, we must decide whether to embrace these novel methods of understanding ourselves and our surroundings.

How augmented cognition will change education and literacy

Augmented cognition, a distinctive branch of artificial intelligence, is characterized by its focus on the synergistic use of AI and human intelligence to address complex challenges. This innovative field leverages AI's capabilities to rapidly enhance the flow of knowledge and data to humans, thereby accelerating learning and problem-solving processes.

Researchers are currently investigating many techniques to bring this concept to fruition. These strategies include utilizing social networks, video games, and digital tools like interactive whiteboards and mobile devices. These elements are integrated across various contexts, from classrooms to individual learners. Nevertheless, this integration must not impede or disrupt the inherent ways humans learn.

Augmented cognition is a form of cognitive enhancement that employs digital technology to bolster brain functionality. This is typically facilitated through computer systems or mobile applications. In contrast to traditional learning models that rely heavily on memorization for subject mastery, augmented cognition can significantly amplify human intellectual capacity by providing instant access to information.

Devices like Google Glass hold immense promise in this context. They could provide students with the information they need precisely when needed, prioritizing necessity over mere convenience. Educators and technologists have been exploring the concept of augmented cognition for over three decades. However, the development of interactive whiteboards and innovative mobile technologies has only recently started to make practical classroom and home applications possible.

As technological advancement continues, the influence and integration of augmented cognition are likely to grow. It may eventually become an intrinsic part of our thinking and learning processes, revolutionizing classrooms and educational methodologies for future generations. The journey toward fully integrated augmented cognition may pose challenges, but it is an exciting frontier that promises to transform how we acquire and apply knowledge.

These cognitive-enhancing tools can also aid in reading, comprehension, and multitasking. But what about children with disabilities? How will this change their learning experience and interaction within classrooms? This question is pertinent since technology has long been employed to assist individuals in overcoming cognitive challenges. For instance, educators are keen to understand how they can apply augmented cognition in a way that does not create barriers to learning for students with disabilities.

Examining how we can integrate augmented cognition into classrooms has proven challenging yet necessary. Educators have recognized that integration must occur without creating additional barriers for individuals with disabilities. Augmented cognition has the potential to reshape our conceptions of intelligence and creativity. Our understanding of learning and what it means to be human are evolving rapidly. Artificial intelligence, machine learning, and brain-computer interfaces are merely a fraction of the list of cognitive enhancement technologies.

Augmented cognition represents the latest frontier in neurotechnology development, capable of significantly enhancing human intellectual capacity through digital technology such as computers or mobile devices and applications. As augmented cognition continues to make us more intelligent, we must consider how our conceptions of intelligence may change. What does a future where humans have unlimited access to information look like?

While we cannot predict the future, augmented cognition is a trend set to expand in the coming years. From what we know about this emerging field of study, individuals proficient in using these technologies will probably think differently than those who do not use them regularly. These techniques will enable augmented cognition to become an integral part of education and literacy in the future, reshaping how we learn, test knowledge, and retain information for lifelong learning.[120] These cognitive enhancement tools are already being integrated into classrooms worldwide. However, the integration is gradual as educators carefully consider incorporating augmented cognition in a way that is not disruptive to natural learning processes.

Integrating augmented cognition into education via AI for digital learning could be a real game changer. It benefits educators and students by providing personalized curricula, responding to individual needs, and encouraging creativity. The future success of our children may hinge on how effectively we leverage these new technologies.

---

[120]. Loveless, B., "Using Augmented Reality in the Classroom" (https://www.educationcorner.com/augmented-reality-classroom-education.html?msclkid=d617ceefa90611ec92c30ca5e3affcfe).

CHAPTER 11

The Future of Education

What kind of future can we envision for our children as AI becomes increasingly integrated into the education system?

Artificial intelligence is fast emerging as a revolutionary educational tool, transforming how we learn and teach. It provides a level of flexibility previously unheard of, allowing students to tailor their learning pace and curriculum according to their needs. Notably, this technology can significantly assist educators in managing diverse classrooms. By assessing individual skill sets, teachers can strategically assign students to projects where their abilities will be most beneficial.

Moreover, AI technology fosters a personalized approach to education. With access to insights about each student's thought processes, teachers can tailor their instruction methods to cater to individual learning styles, enhancing understanding and retention.

While artificial intelligence presents immense potential benefits, striking a balance is crucial. Overreliance on these machines could potentially lead to gaps in learning. To leverage AI in education, we must ensure that it serves as a tool to enhance traditional teaching methods, not replace them. After all, AI should complement human intelligence, not supersede it. The challenge lies in integrating it into our education system to maximize its benefits without compromising essential human interaction and nuanced understanding.

Education around 2030

Indeed, the future is here, and learning has never been more personalized or accessible. As we approach 2030, the impact of AI on education will become more pronounced. Understanding that we are all on unique timelines, individuals can come together to create a customized educational experience.

As we venture into 2030, there will be an increasing demand for jobs in STEM-related fields. Online institutions and programs like Udacity and Khan Academy provide academic and career-focused training that can meet this need. Moreover, prestigious universities such as Stanford, Harvard, and MIT offer free online classes through platforms like EDX, Coursera, and Udemy. These platforms enable anyone to learn complex subjects like quantum mechanics or evolution from the comfort of their homes.

Students increasingly know that STEM fields represent the future, prompting a significant shift toward computer science, engineering, and mathematics careers. From my professional experience, I have observed a growing interest in these fields among students. This change is striking since mathematics was less emphasized during my university years compared to now. It is encouraging to see people becoming more attuned to future demands.

The modernized teaching system offers a variety of tools for students to use at their own pace, anywhere with an internet connection. The rise of internet access has democratized learning, making personalized education common and affordable in our interconnected world.

By 2030, we can expect the world to look quite different. Aspects currently lacking in traditional educational institutions, such as personalized learning and affordable tuition, can be readily accessed online.

The swift transition towards a more technologically connected world leaves many educators contemplating the future of their profession. We stand at the threshold of two eras: one rooted in traditional teaching methods focused on past lessons and another heralding a future where students learn differently. As we prepare for this shift, it is important to embrace change and adapt our teaching methods to meet the evolving needs of tomorrow's learners.

Creativity has become a cornerstone in today's dynamic workforce, driving productivity, innovation, and growth. As Harvard Business School Online suggests, the invention allows employees to work smarter, not harder, thereby enhancing productivity and preventing stagnation in the workplace.[121] Similarly, Calendar.com underscores creativity breeds heightened productivity, increased flexibility, and overall organizational growth.[122]

Students transitioning into this workforce must stay current with the skills employers and global labor markets demand. One such skill that has surged in importance is creativity. While creativity may not have been previously emphasized, its significance has grown exponentially. Therefore, we must equip future generations with innovative ways to express themselves visually and rapidly assemble prototypes when presenting ideas. This not only hones their creative abilities but also prepares them for the evolving demands of the modern job market.

Creativity in the workplace is a multifaceted attribute that offers numerous benefits. It fosters better teamwork, reduces stress, identifies new opportunities, embraces challenges, promotes cognitive development, and improves collaboration.[123,124] Moreover, employee

---

[121]. Boyles M., "The Importance of Creativity in Business" 2022, (https://online.hbs.edu/blog/post/importance-of-creativity-in-business).

[122]. Ritchie, D., "The Importance of Creativity in the Workplace" 2022, (https://www.calendar.com/blog/the-importance-of-creativity-in-the-workplace/).

[123]. Wooll M., "Why Creativity Isn't Just for Creatives and How to Find it Anywhere" 2021, (https://www.betterup.com/blog/creativity-in-the-workplace).

[124]. Indeed Editorial Team. "The Importance of Creativity in Business (Plus Benefits)" 2023, (https://www.indeed.com/career-advice/career-development/importance-of-creativity-in-business).

motivation is critical to creative work. Employees are less likely to generate innovative solutions without engagement and inspiration.[125]

Particularly in a time when algorithms are taking over more and more of our lives, creativity is an irreplaceable human trait. While algorithms excel at programmed tasks, they cannot independently generate innovative ideas or solutions. This is where human creativity outshines, providing the capacity to venture beyond conventional thinking and explore the extraordinary.

Creativity has become essential across various fields, including business, art, and design. The ability to think creatively fuels innovation and provides individuals with a reasonable edge in the workforce. It enables us to constantly seek improvements, overcome challenges, and enhance our lives.

Imagination ignites innovation, guiding us toward fresh ideas and viewpoints that alter how we perceive and engage with the outside world. The process often involves thinking about things in ways we never considered before, pushing the boundaries of what is possible. Thus, fostering creativity is not merely beneficial but crucial for personal development and progress in today's fast-paced world.

LinkedIn emphasizes that creativity involves combining unconventional and unorthodox ideas and solutions, including thinking outside the box and generating unique solutions.[126] However, creativity at work often implies taking risks, which may induce hesitation due to fear of the unknown. Despite these challenges, rewarding creativity communicates value and incentivizes employees to continue thinking innovatively.[127]

---

[125]. Amabile T. and Khaire M., "Creativity and the Role of the Leader" 2008, (https://hbr.org/2008/10/creativity-and-the-role-of-the-leader).

[126]. Poon K., "Why Creativity is Important in the Workplace" 2022, (https://www.linkedin.com/pulse/why-creativity-important-workplace-katy-poon/).

[127]. Betterton K., "How to Foster Creativity in the Workplace" 2023, (https://www.uschamber.com/co/grow/thrive/why-creativity-in-the-workplace-is-so-important).

Fulfilling UNESCO's mission of ensuring equal access to education for all people requires a substantial number of qualified and experienced teachers, particularly at the primary and secondary levels. By 2030, it is estimated that countries will need to hire approximately 68.8 million teachers to provide every child with primary and secondary education. This includes 24.4 million teachers for primary schools and 44.4 million for secondary schools.[128]

An additional challenge arises as many current staff members are expected to leave shortly. Without a contingency plan, this could lead to a critical teacher shortage. Furthermore, there will be a need to find replacements for the 48.6 million teachers projected to retire by 2030. These vacancies will arise from retirements, the conclusion of temporary contracts, or teachers opting for different professions with better pay or working conditions.[129]

Therefore, ensuring a robust pipeline of new teachers and effective retention strategies for existing staff are crucial to meeting these future educational needs. By proactively addressing these challenges, we can work toward UNESCO's goal of universal access to quality education.

Creativity is an inherent skill that can be learned, practiced, and cultivated like any other vocational skill. It allows individuals to embrace innovative approaches, solve problems, and develop innovative ideas. Moreover, it promotes self-expression, boosts mental health, and enhances personal and professional development, making it a valuable asset in various areas of life.

---

[128]. UNESCO Institute of Statistics, 2016. "The World Needs Almost 69 Million New Teachers To Reach the 2030 Education Goals" (http://uis.unesco.org/sites/default/files/documents/fs39-the-world-needs-almost-69-million-new-teachers-to-reach-the-2030-education-goals-2016-en.pdf?msclkid=9ea7d439a91a11ec89f2c248013a4f87).

[129]. Houser, K., "The Solution to Our Education Crisis Might be AI" 2017, (https://futurism.com/ai-teachers-education-crisis).

A world that is smarter than we are

As we contemplate the future, a sense of apprehension often accompanies our thoughts, particularly when pondering the rapid pace of technological advancements. How can we evolve alongside technology when its progress seems to outstrip our adaptability? It is both inspiring and frightening to see society advance so quickly, thanks to technological advancement. Our reliance on technology has permeated almost every facet of life to such an extent that life without it seems unimaginable. However, it raises a critical question: at what point does this dependency start impeding human development? What effects, for instance, will there be if implants or smart pills that offer instant access through neural connections from anywhere in the world replace cell phones?

In today's digital age, reliance on technology has become a common aspect of daily life. This has spurred the development of cutting-edge technologies designed to simplify our lives and enhance the efficiency of routine tasks. As machines evolve in intelligence, they refine their abilities, performing specific tasks more swiftly and economically. But instead of viewing this as a threat, what if we envisage a future where we collaborate with these intelligent machines? Such a perspective fosters a synergy between human creativity and machine efficiency.

Artificial intelligence is revolutionizing the way our society operates, and the field of education is no exception. If educational institutions do not adapt promptly, there is a risk that teachers may lose their pivotal role in shaping the citizens of tomorrow. In an era where AI-powered robots increasingly play significant roles in education, we must redefine our approach.

The call for change in education is not merely due to the advent of chatbots or digital textbooks. We need to equip children with the skills to leverage advancing technologies such as AI to their advantage. These evolving innovations have the potential to profoundly disrupt our society. It operates without human interaction, works flawlessly, and brings intelligence into classrooms that could eventually replace traditional teaching methods.

However, daunting this transition may seem, viewing it as an opportunity rather than a threat is crucial. As technology progresses and becomes more sophisticated, we will inevitably witness the emergence of new educational technologies. To fully integrate AI into the education system, we must advance our understanding and logical thinking about its applications.

While we often consider ourselves the most intelligent beings on Earth, it is vital to remember that a vast universe exists beyond our concerns. Sometimes, we underestimate the extent of human knowledge in technology and innovation, forgetting that the world is far more complex and remarkable than we frequently give it credit for.

There exist countless hidden realms of expertise, mainly unknown to the majority. Some of the most brilliant minds on Earth dedicate their lives to studying these enigmatic subjects, typically with more questions left unanswered than solved. This is a stark reminder of how much we still must learn.

The average person may find it challenging to comprehend the sheer power and intelligence inherent in our planet and its ecosystems. Regularly, people focus on what is directly before them, oblivious to the intricate processes quietly unfolding behind the scenes. This narrow perspective can close our eyes to the broader picture and the extraordinary wonders that our world holds.

Therefore, fostering a sense of curiosity and wonder about the world around us is essential. By doing so, we broaden our horizons, deepen our understanding, and come closer to appreciating our planet's incredible complexity and beauty.

CHAPTER 12

Reflections

There are many misconceptions about the role of artificial intelligence in education. However, a growing body of evidence suggests that AI is already transforming how we learn. The initial section of this discussion highlighted AI's potential benefits and drawbacks, while the subsequent part explored emerging technologies that could positively impact classrooms. As AI tutors actively deliver personalized curricula tailored to each student, student-centered education clearly represents the future of high-performing learning environments.

We anticipate exciting new educational products from startups and industry giants in the coming years. However, it will take some time for educators to adopt AI because of its novelty in the academic setting. The future of education is here, but its distribution remains uneven. It is hoped that the next generation will have access to more innovative learning tools at an earlier age. Though technology is advancing, socioeconomic factors still govern access for many students. Children from wealthier backgrounds, whose parents have sufficient income and time to facilitate home learning, are likely to benefit more than their less privileged peers.

Artificial intelligence can assist teachers in using data to identify students facing learning difficulties and optimize lesson plans accordingly. It could also help manage classrooms by monitoring student behavior and deciding when to intervene. In STEM labs, AI could even control robots, replacing human operators.

Currently, AI has not brought about a radical change in education. Still, we hope this discussion has shed light on how it is already influencing our education system and dispelled some misconceptions about what AI can achieve.

The future of education is fraught with uncertainty. How will students learn? What will become of traditional schools? With technological advancements occurring at an unprecedented pace, how can teachers keep up and create effective lesson plans for a diverse student body with varied interests and learning styles?

Fortunately, the cost of developing AI-powered educational applications has decreased, making it more workable than ever to innovate our teaching methods.

Given the rapid pace of innovation, forecasting the future of education is challenging. Will schools, as we know them, continue to exist? Despite our understanding of current circumstances, it is always difficult to anticipate how educational methods will evolve. However, one thing seems clear—the future of education will increasingly emphasize collaboration. With the popularity of multiplayer online games, many individuals are already accustomed to working on collaborative projects with teammates worldwide.

As we progress through this decade, technological advances are breaking down barriers. The ascent of social media platforms like Instagram, Snapchat, Twitter, and others has revolutionized communication, enabling instant sharing of content across the globe. This presents educators with an exciting opportunity—creating virtual classrooms covering several topics. Furthermore, it raises the question: can students attend classes at times and locations most convenient? Convenience is often an overlooked aspect of education, yet it can significantly impact the quality of learning.

In a world where education is accessible anytime and anywhere, everyone can access quality educational resources, regardless of their circumstances.

Our society is responsible for creating an environment that prepares children for adulthood in a rapidly evolving world. Technological advances are reshaping all aspects of life, including education.

Technology has already altered how students acquire knowledge, progress through the educational system, and interact with teachers and classmates on various platforms. Integrating technology with in-depth student performance analysis will equip learners with the skills they need to thrive in an increasingly digital world.

One of the critical challenges posed by AI in education is ensuring that individuals can keep pace with rapidly evolving technologies while understanding their impact. This will necessitate rethinking traditional teaching methods and placing a greater emphasis on creativity in curriculum development based on innovative technology trends and insights gained from successful and unsuccessful projects.

CHAPTER 13

The concept of effective education is multifaceted and depends on the context and objectives of the teaching situation. However, some universal principles can guide us in becoming better educators.

One of these principles is that good teaching should be student-centered. The teacher must know each student's unique needs and abilities and tailor the instruction accordingly. Another principle is that good teaching requires a solid understanding of the subject matter, allowing the teacher to explain concepts clearly and accurately and help students comprehend how the material interconnects.

Creating a positive and supportive classroom environment is another key element of good teaching. This involves fostering an atmosphere where students feel secure asking questions and making mistakes without fear of ridicule or criticism. Furthermore, good education should be engaging. The teacher must capture the students' interest, make the material relevant to their lives, and stimulate their curiosity. These are just a few components of effective teaching. Becoming a good teacher often involves observing experienced educators and emulating their strategies. Over time and with practice, teachers will develop a unique teaching style that resonates with them and their students.

As we consider the future of education, we must acknowledge the potential role of artificial intelligence (AI). It can challenge teachers to step outside their comfort zones, spurring them to create innovative teaching methods. In today's educational landscape, where classrooms typically lack creativity and innovation, AI can help inspire new possibilities and techniques that could benefit students in the long run.

By incorporating it into our educational processes, human instructors and machines can work together to improve student learning outcomes. It has the potential to enhance engagement and methodology, making it easier for students to learn and retain information. Additionally, it can free up time for instructors, allowing for more one-on-one interaction. It can also provide additional support when teachers need it most. Programmed with knowledge about different learning styles and strategies, AI can assist teachers in customizing their style to meet the distinctive needs of each student. However, it is important to remember that AI is not intended to replace teachers but rather to assist them in providing the best possible education for their students.

Maintaining our quality of life through education requires us to recognize that education is not a static entity but a continually evolving process. We must embrace change and strive to learn and grow continuously. Education is not merely about acquiring knowledge; it is about learning how to apply this knowledge for our benefit and the benefit of others. Therefore, it is not enough to know something; we must also be able to use what we know constructively.

Investing time and effort in both formal learning opportunities and informal learning experiences is essential. If we want to reap the benefits of education, we must be willing to put in the work required to obtain and maintain it.

Understanding that people have different learning styles is crucial in this process. Some may thrive in a structured, formal setting like a classroom or workplace, while others may prefer more informal learning experiences like reading books or engaging in discussions with friends. Furthermore, different individuals may favor visual, auditory, or kinesthetic learning. Recognizing these differences allows us to create a balanced, inclusive educational environment that caters to all learners.

Considering the difference between formal and informal learning, we can feel a balance between structure and freedom. Formal learning provides structure, specific goals, and deadlines, offering a sense of accomplishment and progress that can motivate continued learning. On the other hand, informal learning allows for flexibility and self-paced learning, which can be more enjoyable and engaging. Both learning experiences offer unique benefits, and finding the right balance for each student is critical to effective education.

Identifying the learning preferences of students is indeed crucial to their educational success. There are several ways to discern whether students prefer formal or informal learning environments. One approach is direct inquiry, asking the students about their preferences. However, observations of their behavior and level of engagement in different learning situations can also provide valuable insights.

Students with greater engagement and enthusiasm in structured environments likely lean toward formal education. These learners often thrive on clear instructions, set goals, and a well-defined path to achieving those goals. On the other hand, if a student seems more involved and enthusiastic about less structured, more exploratory learning situations, they may prefer an informal learning approach. Teachers might consider adopting a more facilitative role for these learners, allowing students to explore topics independently and discover knowledge organically.

Educators have the challenging but rewarding task of identifying which learning opportunities best benefit each student. They must create balanced learning environments that incorporate formal and informal learning experiences. This balance allows students to acquire knowledge and develop critical thinking skills, creativity, and a love for lifelong learning.

Ultimately, maintaining our quality of life through education requires a commitment to continuous learning. As society and technology evolve rapidly, we must strive to stay ahead. Embracing lifelong learning ensures we can adapt to changing times, seize new opportunities, and grow personally and professionally.

The goal remains whether we lean towards formal or informal learning: to foster a deep, enduring understanding and love for learning that will serve us throughout our lives.

CHAPTER 14
Solutions for Education with AI

Artificial intelligence is being employed in the classroom, allowing for a more hands-on approach when dealing with students individually. There are many alternative solutions for education today. Computers and AI are becoming more prevalent in the learning process, which has allowed for the realization of personalized data that educators can use to customize their teaching methods. For example, teachers can use neural networks to analyze how students learn best with customized learning plans. These cutting-edge tools and innovations have enabled a more hands-on approach to managing individual students, allowing them to reach their full potential in various subjects and increasing student engagement by taking charge of some aspects of their learning.

Artificial intelligence is making substantial strides in the classroom, enabling a more tailored approach to individual student needs. Computers and AI have become integral to learning in our technologically advanced era. This integration allows for personalized data collection that teachers can utilize to customize their teaching methods. For instance, educators can employ neural networks to analyze students' learning patterns and devise individualized learning plans. With this technology, a more proactive approach toward managing individual students is possible, allowing them to reach their full potential across various subjects. It also encourages students to actively participate in their learning, thereby increasing engagement.

Education is about imparting knowledge and skills and shaping personalities, attitudes, and values. Although AI is already being utilized in education, it is yet to become ubiquitous. As technology evolves rapidly, parents and educators must stay abreast of the latest educational trends.

An important consideration is balancing traditional and contemporary learning methods to provide a comprehensive education. Students should be exposed to conventional forms of learning, such as reading comprehension and mathematics, alongside modern skills like coding. However, striking this balance can be challenging, as students are often thrust into demanding environments where they struggle to keep up.

One potential solution involves offering students a designated number of hours each day to learn in the manner that suits them best, whether through traditional methods or newer ones like coding. For instance, students in a coding class could potentially grasp mathematical concepts more effectively than those who do not participate in such courses. It is a promising approach worth exploring further.

Another way to enhance education is to encourage students to take ownership of their learning. Instead of rote memorization, they could engage in project-based assignments that foster practical skills. These projects could involve creating a stop-motion video demonstrating a process or planning an event. Such activities prepare students for team environments, promoting diversity and collaboration.

To promote successful learning, students must be equipped to handle contradictory or biased information. Schools must provide the necessary equipment for optimal learning, including sufficient laptops and tablets. Fortunately, many companies offer affordable educational packages for schools.

Funding for these resources can come from various sources, including private donors and corporations. The aim is to achieve a high return on investment for every penny spent. Schools must adapt swiftly to keep pace with emerging technologies and trends and offer students diverse post-graduation opportunities.

Schools should offer various courses, ranging from vocational training and arts education to STEM subjects. Opportunities for internships, coding camps, creative writing classes, and blended learning programs should be available. Mentorship programs can help students develop social skills and navigate the workplace. Parental understanding of their child's learning style is crucial for classroom support, including assisting with assignments or finding suitable reading materials. Schools should also establish partnerships with universities, allowing students to graduate with degrees relevant to the modern world.

Schools should expand mental health services by incorporating therapy, medication management, and stress-reducing practices into the curriculum. Activities like yoga, meditation, and mindfulness training can equip students and staff alike with valuable coping skills and resilience. Going beyond traditional academics to support mental wellbeing creates a more compassionate learning environment. With proper training and resources, educators can learn to recognize signs of distress and refer students to the appropriate services. Integrating mental health promotion into the school system fosters psychological, emotional, and social growth alongside intellectual development. This integrated approach allows students to thrive both in and out of the classroom.

Creating a STEM-focused learning environment is essential for the future. Offering classes concentrating on science, technology, engineering, and mathematics allows students to explore these subjects more deeply. Students need to engage with these subjects in exciting and enjoyable ways. With the proper guidance and support, they can acquire the skills they need to succeed in the future.

In summary, a robust education system should integrate both traditional and modern learning methods, promote student ownership of learning, ensure adequate resources, prioritize mental health, and emphasize STEM subjects.

Real-world Educational AI Solutions in use today

AI-based solutions have been in demand for classroom learning, which has prompted software companies to devise tools to aid the educational system. Here are a few of the forerunners in use today that set the pace for further development in the field:

1. Querium

This solution customizes STEM courses to suit students from high school to college. The AI software is programmed to track the total time taken and assess answers for each completed lesson, providing performance insights for teachers and learners.

2. Cognii

Cognii represents multiple AI-powered solutions aimed at tertiary education bodies and corporate training. It is built on a virtual assistant core, allowing it to interact and hold conversations while providing guidelines to boost learners' critical thinking abilities.

3. Blippar

Blippar combines computer vision technology and augmented reality (AR), providing students with the engagement, interactivity, and creativity needed to change learning systems in the classroom. The plan presents interactive visual experiences for biology, physics, and geography. For example, it can render 3D solar system models from traditional textbook images, allowing students to explore the subject with a more direct approach.

4. Nuance

Nuance is a speech recognition system aimed at students who experience trouble with writing. It is fast enough to transcribe about 160 words in a minute. Thus, the inhibitions of typing and spelling that prevent students from achieving their fullest potential are removed.

5. Volley

Volley is a learning platform designed with artificial intelligence at the core of mobile learning, making knowledge management, development, and training more engaging for learners. It assesses students' skill and knowledge gaps and devises individualized tests and courses. Volley can also be used for administrative purposes, including briefing teachers in different disciplines.

6. Kidaptive

Kidaptive achieved popularity for its Adaptive Learning Platform (ALP), which runs on AI algorithms that help colleges and schools pool data, improve learner engagement, and boost outcomes. In addition, it allows for the creation of challenging tests for students targeted at exploring their various weaknesses and strengths.

7. Brainly

Brainly is an online platform for students to share knowledge, collaborate on tasks, and help others. However, instead of following a tech-focused virtual environment, it prioritizes a classroom interface.

8. Quizlet

Quizlet brings variety to the table in terms of study and learning tools. Recently, the solution was updated to include an intelligent study portal designed with adaptive courses for learners. Each study plan is the brainchild of machine learning and data procured from tons of study sessions. Quizlet bridges the gap between relevant and essential materials and students, accurately tackling subjects from multiple angles to avoid ambiguity in knowledge.

9. Thinkster Math

This application is powered by artificial intelligence to tutor students in mathematics. It integrates relevant curriculums into a one-on-one setting to support students in strengthening their math skills through a guided, step-by-step process.

10. Century Tech

Century Tech is well known for its customized learning and teaching plans involving cognitive neuroscience and data analytics. Not only does it relieve the load on teachers, but it also creates personalized lessons for students based on feedback and recommendations.

11. Synthesis

Synthesis is a revolutionary, new early childhood education built for Elon Musk's kids and early engineers at SpaceX to offer a more balanced education. This pioneering program will slowly add more math and science so that it can, in due time, become their fully developed replacement of the legacy K-12 system with physical locations, too, but going digital first. The curriculum for Synthesis can be created by world-class instructors and reach millions of children, which the legacy K–12 system cannot do. Legacy media corporations are encouraged to safeguard the legacy K-12 system, so companies offering an exit from the system must go straight to customers to build their distribution channels. Making an entry easy is a crucial part of the Synthesis strategy, and this is done originally through social media outreach and eschewing legacy media corporations. Ultimately, Synthesis will need physical classrooms to switch to the legacy K–12 system, but this will happen steadily over time as more parents opt into the program.[130,131]

---

130. Srinivasan, B., "Decentralizing Education with Synthesis" 2022, (https://balajis.com/synthesis/).
131. Masad, A., "Investing in Synthesis" 2022, (https://amasad.me/synthesis).

CHAPTER 15

Conclusion

Artificial intelligence can revolutionize education, making it more personalized and accessible than ever before. This technological advancement could pave a fair path for students of all backgrounds and abilities. At this pivotal juncture, we must allow the digital divide to widen or harness innovation to promote equal opportunity, inclusive growth, and economic justice.

As technology evolves, AI will unlock previously unimaginable possibilities. It enables educators to capitalize on each student's unique interests and talents, transforming education from rote learning to a dynamic, lifelong journey. However, integrating AI into education is not without its challenges.

The traditional model of a single human teacher leading a classroom is being redefined. In the future, AI could alleviate teachers' administrative burdens, such as grading exams, freeing them to focus on their primary role—educating students. Yet, this shift toward digitalization, encompassing everything from assessments to communication, brings opportunities and obstacles.

Digitalization has fostered the development of *digital learners*—a significant stride toward modernizing education. Yet while AI-driven individual learning can be beneficial, it might inadvertently stifle creativity and collaborative problem-solving skills, vital components of holistic education.

We must tread carefully as we navigate toward a future where AI plays a more significant role in education. While it is unlikely that AI will fully replace teachers shortly, it has already significantly altered many aspects of our lives and work. We must be prepared to address the long-term implications of this shift, including the potential for job displacement among educators.

Educators must understand the disruptive power of AI. In recent years, numerous software-related jobs have been automated due to advancements in AI. This immensely pressures teachers to increase efficiency and extend their working hours. Before introducing AI into classrooms, schools must ensure they have a robust system, and that support is available to help students navigate this AI-driven world.

Education is a vibrant realm brimming with potential. As we delve deeper into this intriguing world, I sincerely hope we approach it positively and enrichingly for all stakeholders. By doing so, we can ensure that integrating AI into education results in a more engaging, personalized, and effective learning experience for all students.

BIBLIOGRAPHY

Strickland, E., "The turbulent past and uncertain future of Artificial Intelligence" 2021, (https://spectrum.ieee.org/history-of-ai).

Musk, E., "Joe Rogan Experience" #1470, 2020, J. Rogan, Interviewer.

Narrow Artificial Intelligence, "What is Narrow Artificial Intelligence (Narrow AI)?" Definition from Techopedia, 2022, (https://www.techopedia.com/definition/32874/narrow-artificial-intelligence-narrow-ai#:~:text=Narrow%20artificial%20intelligence%20%28narrow%20AI%29%20is%20a%20specific,will%20not%20automatically%20be%20applied%20to%20other%20tasks).

Machine Learning Knowledge, "5 Epic Times when AI defeated Human Champions in Games" 2019, (https://machinelearningknowledge.ai/epic-times-when-ai-defeated-humans-champions-in-games/).

Senior, J. and Gyarmathy, É., AI and Developing Human Intelligence, (2 Park Square, Milton Park, Abingdon, Oxon OX14 4RN: Routledge, 2022), p. 81.

Trappl, R., "Programs can do everything that humans can - and more" 2015, Futurezone, Interviewer.

Wikipedia.org, "Stanford-Binet Intelligence Scales" 2021, (https://en.wikipedia.org/wiki/Stanford%E2%80%93Binet_Intelligence_Scales).

Ranjha, A., "Intelligence Test – An Overview of Stanford-Binet Intelligence Test" (https://psychologyroots.com/intelligence-test-an-overview-of-stanford-binet-intelligence-test/).

Whitten, A., "Do IQ. Tests Actually Measure Intelligence?" 2020, (https://www.discovermagazine.com/mind/do-iq-tests-actually-measure-intelligence).

Hamsher, K., "Intelligence and Aphasia" 2007, (https://doi.org/10.1016/B978-012619322-0/50013-0).

Darwin, C. "The origin of species by means of natural selection, or the preservation of favored races in the struggle for life. In C. Darwin, the origin of species by means of natural selection, or the preservation of favored races in the struggle for life." (London: John Murray, 1872), p. 181.

Harari, Y. N., Sapiens: A Brief History of Humankind. (Signal Books, 2014), p.35.

"Education and training in Europe: inequality remains a challenge" Brussels: European Commission, 2017, (https://ec.europa.eu/commission/presscorner/detail/en/IP_17_4261).

Media & Learning, "Europe's Budget for Education and Training at Its Lowest" 2020, (https://media-and-learning.eu/type/news/europes-budget-for-education-and-training-at-its-lowest/).

Lifelong Learning Platform (LLLP), "Europe's share of GDP for education and training has never been this low. A comparative analysis" 2020, (https://lllplatform.eu/news/europes-share-of-gdp-for-education-and-training-has-never-been-this-low-a-comparative-analysis-investment-education-eurostat/).

"The Europeanization of schooling: what is a European Education?" OpenDemocracy Press, 2018, (https://www.opendemocracy.net/en/can-europe-make-it/europeanization-of-schooling/).

Sunstrom, L., "School is for Fools: 10 Reasons the Education System is a Failure" 2019, (https://startgainingmomentum.com/school-fools-10-reasons-education-system-failure/).

Lynch, M., "20 Reasons Why the American Education System is Failing" The Tech Edvocate, 2021, (https://www.thetechedvocate.org/20-reasons-why-the-american-education-system-is-failing/).

Nelson, L., "America spends more than $600 billion on schools. Here's where it goes and why it matters" 2015, (https://www.vox.com/2015/3/25/8284637/school-spending-US).

Camera, L., "Biden's Budget Significantly Boosts K-12 Education Spending" 2021, (https://www.usnews.com/news/education-news/articles/2021-04-09/bidens-budget-significantly-boosts-k-12-education-spending).

García E. and Weiss E., "US schools struggle to hire and retain teachers. The second report in 'The Perfect Storm in the Teacher Labor Market' series" 2019, (https://www.epi.org/publication/u-s-schools-struggle-to-hire-and-retain-teachers-the-second-report-in-the-perfect-storm-in-the-teacher-labor-market-series/).

"US children and teens spend more time on academics" (University Michigan Press, 2004, https://news.umich.edu/u-s-children-and-teens-spend-more-time-on-academics/).

American Heart Association, "Many Teens Spend 30 Hours A Week On 'Screen Time' During High School" 2008, (https://www.sciencedaily.com/releases/2008/03/080312172614.htm).

McCormick, Alexander C., It's About Time: What to Make of Reported Declines in How Much College Students Study Association of American Colleges & Universities Liberal Education, (Win 2011, https://www.aacu.org/publications-research/periodicals/its-about-time-what-make-reported-declines-how-much-college), v97 n1 p30–39.

Welch, A., "Health experts say parents need to drastically cut kids' screen time" CBS News, 2018, (https://www.cbsnews.com/news/parents-need-to-drastically-cut-kids-screen-time-devices-american-heart-association/).

Rishi Bommasani, Drew A. Hudson, E., On the Opportunities and Risks of Foundation Models. Center for Research on Foundation Models (CRFM), (Cornell University Press, 2021).

ActiveLearn, 2021, (https://www.pearsonactivelearn.com/app/Home).

"AI Will Power 95% Of Customer Interactions By 2025" Finance Digest Press (https://www.financedigest.com/ai-will-power-95-of-customer-interactions-by-2025.html).

Amazon Web Services, Inc., 2021, Alexa in Education (https://aws.amazon.com/education/alexa-edu/).

Quintero, J., Baldiris, S., Rubira, R., Cerón J. & Velez, G., "Augmented Reality in Educational Inclusion. A Systematic Review on the Last" Frontiers in Psychology Decade, 2019, (https:// doi: 10.3389/fpsyg.2019.01835).

Kahoot.com, 2021, (https://kahoot.com/).

Papanastasiou, G.P., Drigas, A., Skianis, C. and Lytras M., "Virtual and augmented reality effects on K-12, higher and tertiary education students' twenty-first-century skills" (https:// doi:10.1007/s10055-018-0363-2).

"Augmented reality in education: teaching tool or passing trend" The Guardian Press, 2013, (https://www.theguardian.com/higher-education-network/blog/2013/feb/11/augmented-reality-teaching-tool-trend).

Alsop, T., "Global mobile augmented reality (AR) users 2024" Statista, 2021, (https://www.statista.com/statistics/1098630/global-mobile-augmented-reality-ar-users/).

Papanastasiou, G.P., Drigas, A., Skianis, C., and Lytras M., "Virtual and augmented reality effects on K-12, higher and tertiary education students' twenty-first-century skills" (https://doi:10.1007/s10055-018-0363-2).

Romereborn.org, 2021, (https://www.romereborn.org/).

Bentley, P., "What is artificial intelligence?" BBC Science Focus Magazine, 2020, (https://www.sciencefocus.com/future-technology/artificial-intelligence-ai/?msclkid=2250883da76011ecaecbb1a9a157b6be).

Sears, K., "STEM Education Innovation Lab Partners with Gwinnett County Schools to Offer Innovative AgSTEM Learning Experience" 2020, (https://den.mercer.edu/stem-education-innovation-lab-partners-with-gwinnett-county-schools-to-offer-innovative-agstem-learning-experience/?msclkid=16ad6606a76111eca5d5f1a01c26ceb8).

Luna, H., "How AI will Completely Transform Education" Digital Trends, 2017, (https://blogs.csun.edu/aix/2017/09/28/how-ai-will-completely-transform-education-digital-trends/?msclkid=759e3ff6a7a911eca1d2b68b773d84f3).

Hudson, H., "20 Educational Games and Activities for Alexa" 2020, (https://www.weareteachers.com/educational-alexa-skills/?msclkid=1f34ec5da7aa11ecba6f1f039a07aa7e).

Business Insider. "'What is the Amazon Echo Dot?': Everything you need to know about Amazon's compact smart speaker" 2021, (https://www.businessinsider.com/what-is-amazon-echo-dot).

Greenwald D.,2023, "Amazon Echo Dot (5th Gen, 2022 Release) Review, https://www.pcmag.com/reviews/amazon-echo-dot-5th-gen

Skype.com. 2021, (https://www.skype.com/en/).

Hangouts.google.com. 2021, (https://hangouts.google.com/).

Smith-Robbins, S. "Higher Education as Virtual Conversation" EDUCAUSE Review, vol. 43, no. 5, 2008, (https://er.educause.edu/articles/2008/9/higher-education-as-virtual-conversation?msclkid=cde9392da82b11eca4cf34cc2f1016bb).

Wallace, P. and Marryott, J., "The impact of avatar self-representation on collaboration in virtual worlds" Journal of Online Education, 5 (5), 2009, (1–6).

Holz, S., "How AI is changing special education" 2017, (https://blog.neolms.com/ai-changing-special-education/).

Artificial Intelligence Research, "Neural Network Shows People with Autism Read Expressions Differently" Tohoku University, 2021, (https://www.onartificialintelligence.com/articles/24463/neural-network-shows-people-with-autism-read-expressions-differently).

2016. "AI glasses help children with autism read facial expressions" Springwise, 2016, (https://www.springwise.com/ai-glasses-helps-children-autism-read-facial-expressions/).

Solomon, O., "The uses of technology for and with children with Autism Spectrum Disorders" 2012, (https://www.researchgate.net/publication/281067142_The_uses_of_technology_for_and_with_children_with_Autism_Spectrum_Disorders).

Design Indaba, "Smart glasses help kids with autism recognize facial expressions and emotions" 2018, Retrieved from (https://anotherlightup.designindaba.com/articles/creative-work/smart-glasses-help-kids-autism-recognise-facial-expressions-and-emotions?msclkid=6301fd30a7ad11ecb2b5a3dd03bfcaa8).

Querium (http://querium.com/).

Schroer, A., "AI In Education: 12 Companies You Should Know" 2018, Updated 2022, (https://builtin.com/artificial-intelligence/ai-in-education).

CENTURY English, Maths, and Science, 2022, (https://www.century.tech/?msclkid=07ced7e9a7b211eca2febeb346a855fc).

Aieducator.2021, (https://aieducator.com/).

Khan Academy, 2021, (https://www.khanacademy.org/).

Duolingo, 2021, Learn a language for free (https://www.duolingo.com/).

Coursera, 2021, "Online Courses & Credentials from Top Educators" 2021 (https://www.coursera.org/).

Official Rosetta Stone® 2021, Language Learning - Learn a Language (https://www.rosettastone.com/).

TensorFlow 2021, (https://www.tensorflow.org/).

Marr, B., "How Is AI Used in Education—Real World Examples of Today and a Peek into the Future" Forbes, 2018, (https://www.forbes.com/sites/bernard-marr/2018/07/25/how-is-ai-used-in-education-real-world-examples-of-today-and-a-peek-into-the-future/?sh=184e8b0b586e).

Smith A. and Anderson, J. "Predictions for the State of AI and Robotics in 2025" Pew Research Center, 2014, (https://www.pewresearch.org/internet/2014/08/06/predictions-for-the-state-of-ai-and-robotics-in-2025/).

Tuomi, Ilkka, "The Impact of Artificial Intelligence on Learning, Teaching, and Education" 2018, (https:/doi:10.2760/12297).

Brynjolfsson, Erik and Andrew McAfee, The Second Machine Age: Work, Progress, and Prosperity in a Time of Brilliant Technologies (New York City: W. W. Norton & Company, 2014).

Willis, P., "Should Computers Replace Teachers in Class?" 2019, (https://study.com/blog/should-computers-replace-teachers-in-class.html).

Tazrout, Z., "Voice analysis on a smartphone to detect signs of a depressive disorder Actu IA" 2021, (https://www.bing.com/search?q=Voice+analysis+on+a+smartphone+to+detect+signs+of+a+depressive+disorder+-+Actu+IA&cvid=30dab38c452a45639ecd0c9a19c4f26f&aqs=edge..69i57j69i60.628j0j4&FORM=ANAB01&PC=LCTS).

Fagherazzi, G., Fischer, A., Ismael,M. and Despotovic, V., Voice for Health: The Use of Vocal Biomarkers from Research to Clinical Practice Digital Biomarkers 2021, Vol. 5, No. 1, (Karger Publishers, https:// doi: 10.1159/000515346).

Nuffield Foundation "More teachers are reporting mental health problems than ever" 2020, (https://www.nuffieldfoundation.org/news/more-teachers-reporting-mental-health-problems-than-ever).

University College London, "More teachers reporting mental health problems" 2020, (https://www.ucl.ac.uk/news/2020/jan/more-teachers-reporting-mental-health-problems).

Cherry, K., Cognitive Behavioral Therapy (CBT): Definition, Types, Techniques, Efficiency, 2021, (https://www.verywellmind.com/what-is-cognitive-behavior-therapy-2795747).

LaFrance, A. "Machines That Can See Depression on a Person's Face" 2015, (https://www.theatlantic.com/technology/archive/2015/10/machines-that-can-see-depression-on-a-persons-face/411229/).

Venkataraman, D., Parameswaran, N. "Extraction of Facial Features for Depression Detection among Students" International Journal of Pure and Applied Mathematics 2018, Volume 118 No. 7 2018, p. 455–463, Retrieved from (https://acad-publ.eu/jsi/2018-118-7-9/articles/7/61.pdf?msclkid=17b11eb8a83211ec85105e2f409d223f).

"Machine learning and financial institutions" VISA CONSULTING & ANALYTICS, 2019, (https://all-lb.visa.com/partner-with-us/visa-consulting-analytics/machine-learning-and-financial-institutions.html).

IBM "What is Computer Vision?" (https://www.ibm.com/topics/computer-vision?msclkid=7fa75259a82811ec87bc171eeb2bde4a).

Pedró, F., Subosa, M., Rivas, A., "Artificial intelligence in education: challenges and opportunities for sustainable development" UNESCO Digital Library, 2019, (https://unesdoc.unesco.org/ark:/48223/pf0000366994).

MOOC.org. Massive Open Online Courses An edX Site (https://www.mooc.org/).

Marr, B., "How Is AI Used in Education—Real World Examples of Today and a Peek Into the Future" Forbes, 2018, (https://www.forbes.com/sites/bernard-marr/2018/07/25/how-is-ai-used-in-education-real-world-examples-of-today-and-a-peek-into-the-future/?sh=184e8b0b586e).

Ahmed, H., "Challenges of AI and Data Privacy—And How to Solve Them" 2021, (https://www.isaca.org/resources/news-and-trends/newsletters/atisaca/2021/volume-32/challenges-of-ai-and-data-privacy-and-how-to-solve-them).

Abinisha S., "AI Detect individual's mood by analyzing speech" 2017, (https://abinisha444com.wordpress.com/2017/02/05/ai-detect-individuals-mood-by-analysing-speech-5/?mscl-kid=448fec35a83511ec92cbc53f93333b48).

Smith, D., "Capturing the Sound of Depression in the Human Voice" 2017, (https://www.kqed.org/futureofyou/435986/capturing-the-sound-of-depression-in-the-human-voice).

Facebook, 2021, (https://www.facebook.com/).

Kesari, G., "AI Can Now Detect Depression from Your Voice, and It's Twice as Accurate as Human Practitioners" 2021, (https://www.forbes.com/sites/ganeskesari/2021/05/24/ai-can-now-detect-depression-from-just-your-voice/?sh=781e8c834c8d).

Stevens Institute of Technology, "Detecting Depression, Using AI" 2021, (https://www.stevens.edu/news/detecting-depression-using-ai).

Datta, D., Majumdar, S., Sen, O., International Journal of Innovative Technology and Exploring Engineering (IJITEE), Volume 9 Issue 2, December 2019, (https://doi: 10.35940/ijitee. B6158.129219).

Datta, D., Roy, A., Datta, S., Roy, U., International Journal of Soft Computing and Engineering, Volume 8 Issue 6, August 2019, (https:// doi: 10.35940/ijeat. F7987.088619).

Torres, B., Simões, P., Sousa, M., Santos, R., "Facial Expression Recognition in Alzheimer's Disease: a Longitudinal Study" 2014, (https://doi:10.1590/0004-282X20150009).

American Psychological Association, "Beck Depression Inventory (BDI)" 2020, Updated 2021, (https://www.apa.org/pi/about/publications/caregivers/practice-settings/assessment/tools/beck-depression).

"11 Facts About High School Dropout Rates" (https://www.dosomething.org/us/facts/11-facts-about-high-school-dropout-rates).

Paulson, A., "Fewer US schools qualify as 'dropout factories'" 2021, (https://www.csmonitor.com/USA/Education/2011/0322/Fewer-US-schools-qualify-as-dropout-factories).

Mashhad, M., "Combatting School Dropout in Europe United Way Worldwide" 2021, (https://www.unitedway.org/blog/combatting-school-dropout-in-europe#).

"UNESCO: 264 million children do not go to school" 2017, (https://www.dw.com/en/unesco-264-million-children-dont-go-to-school/a-41084932).

American University, "5 Ways Policy Makers Can Improve the Quality of Education" 2019, (https://soeonline.american.edu/blog/5-ways-policy-makers-can-improve-the-quality-of-education).

Snow, J., "People with Disabilities Are Using AI to Improve Their Lives" 2019, (https://www.pbs.org/wgbh/nova/article/people-with-disabilities-use-ai-to-improve-their-lives/?msclkid=8e744bd4a87811ec93c08d26ab07082).

Utermohlen K., "4 Applications of Artificial Intelligence for Hearing Loss"
2018, (https://medium.com/@karl.utermohlen/4-applications-of-artificial-intelligence-for-hearing-loss-64f3e189847e).

IndustryWired. "Top 7 AI Tools to Battle Against Hearing Impairment" 2021, (https://industrywired.com/top-7-ai-tools-to-battle-against-hearing-impairment/).

Burry M., "Hearing aids with Artificial Intelligence" 2021, (https://www.healthyhearing.com/report/53168-Hearing-aids-artificial-intelligence-deep-learning-oticon).

Asokan A. "5 Ways in Which AI Is Improving Accessibility for the Hearing Impairment" 2019, (https://analyticsindiamag.com/5-ways-in-which-ai-is-improving-accessibility-for-the-hearing-impaired/).

Department of Human Services Minnesota, "Apps for Hearing Loss" (https://mn.gov/deaf-hard-of-hearing/assistive-technology/apps/).

Chung G., "Five New Partnerships to Shape the Future of Hearing Technology" 2023, (https://blog.google/intl/en-au/company-news/technology/ai-hearing-initiative/).

Research Impact, "Voicebox: Facilitating Science Teaching in Schools" 2014,
(https://www.ucl.ac.uk/impact/case-studies/2014/dec/voicebox-facilitating-science-teaching-schools).

JR Raphael, "16 Ways Google Lens Can Make You More Productive on Android" Computerworld, 2023, (https://www.computerworld.com/article/3572639/google-lens.html).

Artificial Intelligence - Office of Educational Technology (https://tech.ed.gov/ai/).

"Artificial Intelligence in Educa-
    tion" (https://www.unesco.org/en/digital-education/artifi-
    cial-intelligence).
Chen C., "AI Will Transform Teaching and Learning. Let's Get It
    Right" 2023, (https://hai.stanford.edu/news/ai-will-trans-
    form-teaching-and-learning-lets-get-it-right).
International Journal of Artificial Intelligence in Education, 2023,
    (https://www.springer.com/journal/40593).
University of San Diego, "43 Examples of Artificial Intelligence in
    Education" (https://onlinedegrees.sandiego.edu/artificial-in-
    telligence-education/).
Phillips V., "Intelligent Classrooms: What AI Means for the Future
    of Education" 2023,
    (https://www.forbes.com/sites/vickiphillips/2023/06/07/in-
    telligent-classrooms-what-ai-means-for-the-future-of-edu-
    cation/).
"AI Exploration for Educators: Putting Educators and Students in
    the Driver's Seat" (https://www.iste.org/areas-of-focus/AI-
    in-education).
Marr B., "How Is AI Used in Education—Real World Examples of
    Today and a Peek into the Future" (https://bernard-
    marr.com/how-is-ai-used-in-education-real-world-examples-
    of-today-and-a-peek-into-the-future/).
Anderson J., Harvard EdCast "Educating in a World of Artificial In-
    telligence" 2023, (https://www.gse.harvard.edu/ideas/ed-
    cast/23/02/harvard-edcast-educating-world-artificial-intelli-
    gence).
Hardesty G., "AI That Teaches Other AI" 2023,
    (https://viterbischool.usc.edu/news/2023/07/teaching-ro-
    bots-to-teach-other-robots/).
Sweezy T., "AI Study Finds Robots Can Learn From Each Other
    Just Like Humans" 2023, (https://hothardware.com/news/ai-
    study-finds-robots-learn-from-each-other).

Bild N., "AI Goes Back to School" 2023, (https://www.hackster.io/news/ai-goes-back-to-school-828d17db7c45).

Rhem A., "The Connection between Artificial Intelligence and Knowledge Management" 2017, (https://www.kminstitute.org/blog/connection-between-artificial-intelligence-and-knowledge-management).

Jarrahi M., Askay D., Eshraghi A., and Smith P., "Artificial Intelligence and Knowledge Management: A Partnership Between Human and AI" 2022, (https://www.sciencedirect.com/science/article/pii/S0007681322000222).

Çitak E., "Collaboration Sparks the Flames of Machine Learning" 2023, (https://dataconomy.com/2023/07/17/shared-learning-peer-to-peer-learning/).

Woodall T., "Overcoming 'Catastrophic Forgetting': A Leap in AI Continuous Learning" Neuroscience News, 2023, (https://neurosciencenews.com/ai-continuous-learning-23671/).

Quora, "What is Static General Knowledge?" (https://www.quora.com/What-is-static-general-knowledge?msclkid=af39a04da90511ecaea1edcd381f47c9).

Wikipedia, "Dynamic knowledge repository" (https://en.wikipedia.org/wiki/Dynamic_knowledge_repository).

Wikipedia, "Augmented cognition" (https://en.wikipedia.org/wiki/Augmented_cognition#:~:text=Augmented%20cognition.%20Augmented%20cognition%20is%20an%20interdisciplinary%20area,and%20environments%20where%20human%E2%80%93computer%20interaction%20and%20interfaces%20?msclkid=e917W6a4ca90511ecb715e2eb99193ea9).

Loveless, B., "Using Augmented Reality in the Classroom" (https://www.educationcorner.com/augmented-reality-classroom-education.html?msclkid=d617ceefa90611ec92c30ca5e3affcfe).

Boyles M., "The Importance of Creativity in Business" 2022, (https://online.hbs.edu/blog/post/importance-of-creativity-in-business).

Ritchie, D., "The Importance of Creativity in the Workplace" 2022, (https://www.calendar.com/blog/the-importance-of-creativity-in-the-workplace/).

Wooll M., "Why creativity isn't just for creatives and how to find it anywhere" 2021, (https://www.betterup.com/blog/creativity-in-the-workplace).

Indeed Editorial Team, "The Importance of Creativity in Business (Plus Benefits)" 2023, (https://www.indeed.com/career-advice/career-development/importance-of-creativity-in-business).

Amabile T., Khaire M., "Creativity and the Role of the Leader" 2008, (https://hbr.org/2008/10/creativity-and-the-role-of-the-leader).

Belsky, S., "What professional skills will be the most important in the future?" World Economic Forum, 2020, (https://www.weforum.org/agenda/2020/11/ai-automation-creativity-workforce-skill-fute-of-work).

Poon K., "Why Creativity is Important in the Workplace" 2022, (https://www.linkedin.com/pulse/why-creativity-important-workplace-katy-poon/).

Betterton K., "How to Foster Creativity in the Workplace" 2023, (https://www.uschamber.com/co/grow/thrive/why-creativity-in-the-workplace-is-so-important).

UNESCO Institute of Statistics, "The World Needs Almost 69 Million New Teachers To Reach the 2030 Education Goals" 2016, (http://uis.unesco.org/sites/default/files/documents/fs39-the-world-needs-almost-69-million-new-teachers-to-reach-the-2030-education-goals-2016-en.pdf?msclkid=9ea7d439a91a11ec89f2c248013a4f87).

Houser, K., "The Solution to Our Education Crisis Might be AI" 2017, (https://futurism.com/ai-teachers-education-crisis).

Schroer, A., "AI In Education: 11 Companies You Should Know"
    2018, (https://builtin.com/artificial-intelligence/ai-in-educa-
    tion).
Srinivasan, B., "Decentralizing Education with Synthesis" 2022,
    (https://balajis.com/synthesis/).
Masad, A., "Investing in Synthesis" 2022, (https://amasad.me/syn-
    thesis).

Ingrid Seabra boasts an international career spanning finance, pharmaceuticals, and education. She began as a credit risk analyst at Barclays Bank in London, gaining invaluable experience in the global banking sector. Her strong analytical skills led her to a role as a statistician for the European Central Bank (ECB) in Germany, where she contributed statistical analysis to guide Eurozone economic policy.

Eager to apply her quantitative talents more directly, Ingrid became a senior biostatistician at BIAL Pharmaceuticals in Portugal. She made key statistical contributions, leading to several published medical studies during her time there. Today, Ingrid channels her passion for statistics and mathematics as an educator and consultant. She develops academic curricula and provides tailored training for students, equipping them with the analytical skills needed to excel in various mathematics exams and gain entry to top universities worldwide.

Ingrid is also a researcher exploring how to optimize learning through AI technology. With her multidisciplinary background and international perspective, Ingrid brings a wealth of experience to her educational programs and research. Her focus on mathematics, technology, and global experiences provides her with unique insights to share as an educator.

For more information about Ingrid Seabra and her work, please visit her website at www.ingridseabra.com, and you are welcome to get in touch via email at hello@ingridseabra.com.

BRIDGING TOMORROW'S KNOWLEDGE GAP WITH AI

For more information about Ingrid Seabra and her work, please visit her website at www.ingridseabra.com, and you are welcome to get in touch via email at hello@ingridseabra.com.

171

Publications by Ingrid Seabra

Conversas com a Inteligencia Artificial: 111 Perguntas

Conversas com a Inteligência Artificial

Let's Ask AI

A Inteligência Artificial e o Futuro da Educação